Taking the Leap

**Building a Career
as a Visual Artist**

Taking the Leap

Cay Lang

CHRONICLE BOOKS

SAN FRANCISCO

Every effort has been made to track down permissions in this book. If something has been overlooked, please alert the publisher. We are grateful to the artists, collectors, museums, galleries, and agents who granted us permission to reprint the following works:
Page 1. Illustration by Richard Stine. © 1994 Richard Stine. Page 23. *Back of Painting of Mount Slope.* © 1992 Edward Gorey. Reprinted by permission of Parnassus Imprints, Inc. Page 55. Drawing by R. Chast. © 1995 The New Yorker Magazine, Inc. Page 64. Calvin and Hobbes © 1992 Watterson. Dist. By Universal Press Syndicate. Reprinted with permission. All rights reserved. Page 84. Drawing by Ziegler. © 1996 The New Yorker Magazine, Inc. Page 101. Drawing by Sempé. © 1984 The New Yorker Magazine, Inc. Page 123. Drawing by M. Stevens. © 1984 The New Yorker Magazine, Inc. Page 144. *Masterpiece 1962.* © Roy Lichtenstein. Page 160. Illustration by Richard Stine. © 1994 Richard Stine.

Taking the Leap, a professional practices program for artists, can be reached by telephone at 510 653-1655 or on the web at www.takingtheleap.com.

Library of Congress Cataloging-in-Publication Data:
Lang, Cay.
 Taking the leap : building a career as a visual artist / by Cay Lang.
 224 p.   17.8 x 23.4 cm.
 Includes index.
 ISBN 0-8118-1815-2
 1. Art—Vocational guidance.   I. Title.
N8350.L36   1998
702'.3—dc21   97-41038
                                                   CIP

Printed in the United States of America.

Cover design by Liz Rico
Cover illustration copyright © 1998 by Andrew Faulkner
Interior design by Amy Evans McClure

Distributed in Canada by Raincoast Books
8680 Cambie Street
Vancouver, British Columbia V6P 6M9

10 9 8 7 6 5 4 3 2

Chronicle Books
85 Second Street
San Francisco. California 94105

www.chroniclebooks.com

For my father, Robert Lang,
and for my mother, Loraine Lang

Contents

Preface

As an artist just starting out, I was full of the excitement and intense terror that afflicts any traveler embarking on a journey to unknown shores where the inhabitants are rumored to be cannibals. Happily, after having lived in those once-foreign lands for many years, and after countless hours of arranging exhibitions and dealing with galleries, collectors, museums, critics, and publications, I can honestly report that although the excitement remains, the terror is gone. People are people, and art, as it turns out, is an ever-renewing spring, always fresh and clear. Gilbert and George once said, "To be with art is all I ask," and I, gratefully, agree.

When I first started exhibiting my art, straight out of art school, there were no signposts to help me find my way to becoming successful. Art schools do a great job of teaching artists about art, and a half-hearted to nonexistent job of teaching artists about the business of being an artist. I had to learn by trial and error (well, more by trial and error and error and error), and it took almost ten years before I really understood the fundamentals of how the art world worked. The art world is not all that complicated; part of the problem is that much of the interaction goes on behind closed doors and thus remains shrouded in mystery, and part of the problem lies in the fact that each character in the story can only see the plot from his or her point of view.

As my art career unfolded, from showing in nonprofit spaces, to national gallery representation and publication in books and magazines, and eventually to being seen in international museums and galleries, I picked up more pieces of the puzzle. By 1990, I had been teaching photography to university students for some time, and every new batch of students would ask me, "How can we get our work seen and sold?" The answer was too complex for a ten-minute conversation, or even a semester's-length class, so I started the Taking the Leap program, condensing ten years of information picked up in the trenches into an intense six-month practicum.

The class was designed to be effective. I didn't want to create yet another situation where students dutifully attended a class, took great notes, and then filed them away somewhere for future use. I wanted things actually to happen for the students in a measurable way. I wanted them to experience the thrill of metamorphosis from art student to professional artist within the time line of the class itself, and I wanted to be there to hear them come bouncing in to announce that they just sold their first piece, or got their first show, or won an award. I decided the class should meet weekly for no less than six months, limited the enrollment to twelve, and interviewed the students ahead of time to determine whether or not they were ready to market their work. The class turned out to be amazingly affirmative, with a high percentage of the artists going on to international art careers.

This book is designed to recreate as closely as possible the experience of the class. In a classroom situation, there is a lot of give and take: people ask questions, they get answers, people question the answers, other people question the questions. By the time we get through, everyone has a thorough understanding of the topic—not just How Things Are Done, but how the art world got that way, how it is changing, and what the options are. Creative people rarely want to follow rules, but my feeling is that if you know what is behind the rules, you can make intelligent decisions about how to use them, or change them if you like.

I am grateful for the numerous colleagues and friends without

The object isn't to make art, it's to be in that wonderful state which makes art inevitable.

ROBERT HENRI

whose support, knowledge, and generosity this book would not have been possible. It really does take a legion of contributors to make a book. I am especially grateful for the insider information so many busy art professionals unselfishly shared in the research and on the writing of this book: M. C. Anderson, of MC Gallery, Minneapolis; Paule Anglim, of Gallery Paule Anglim, San Francisco; Robert Brown, of the Robert Brown Gallery, Washington D.C.; Roy Boyd, of Roy Boyd Gallery, Chicago; Rosamund Felson, of Rosamund Felson Gallery, Santa Monica; Kim Foster, of the Kim Foster Gallery, New York; Gail Gibson, of G. Gibson Gallery, Seattle; Allene LaPides, of Allene LaPides Gallery, Santa Fe; Roberta Lieberman, of Zolla/Lieberman Gallery, Chicago; Benjamin Mangel, of Mangel Gallery, Philadelphia; Carolyn Miles, of Atrium Gallery, Saint Louis; Richard Nesbitt, of D.O.C.S. Gallery, New Orleans; Christine Normile, of Sherry Frumkin Gallery, Santa Monica; Janelle Reiring, of Metro Pictures, New York; Christopher Schmidt, of Schmidt/Dean Gallery, Philadelphia; Holly Solomon, of Holly Solomon Gallery, New York; Allan Stone, of Allan Stone Gallery, New York; Jeremy Stone, dealer/educator, San Francisco; Martha Wilson, of Franklin Furnace Archive, Inc., New York.

Then there are the wonderful people whose insights have enriched the development of the program itself, whose experiences, generously shared, have added depth and color: Amy Berk, art critic; Bill Berkson, art critic for *Artforum Magazine*; Janet Bishop, curator at the San Francisco Museum of Modern Art; David Bonetti, art critic for the *San Francisco Examiner;* Frish Brandt, director of the Fraenkel Gallery; Jamie Brunson, artist and critic; Catharine Clark, of the Catharine Clark Gallery; Terri Cohn, writer/curator; Rene de Guzman, from the Yerba Buena Center for the Arts; John Delois, director of Space 743; Rene di Rosa, founder of the Di Rosa Art Preserve; Michael Floss, director of the Business Volunteers for the Arts; Marnie Gillette, director of SF Camerawork Gallery; Jo Hanson, artist; Kim Harrington, photographer; Robbin Henderson, director of the Berkeley Art Center; Jo Leggett, editor of *Photo Metro* magazine; Carrie Lederer, painter; Leah Levy, independent curator; Mark Levy, art historian; Suzy Locke, art consultant; Vance Martin, private art dealer; Lydia Matthews, art historian; Robert McDonald, independent curator; Judy Moran, curator, San Francisco Arts Commission; Douglas Nickel, associate curator of photography at the San Francisco Museum of Modern Art; Marian Parmenter, director of the San Francisco Museum of Modern Art Rental Gallery; Stephen Pon, painter; Maria Porges, artist; Renny Pritikin, art director, Yerba Buena Center for the Arts; Harry Roche, art critic, San Francisco *Bay Guardian*; Joan Roebuck, of the Joan Roebuck Gallery; Chiori Santiago, art critic; Michael Shapiro, of the Michael Shapiro Gallery; Michaeline Stankus, art advisor; Elizabeth Sunday, photographer; Michael Schwager, director, Sonoma State University Gallery; Jason Tannen, artist; Tim Taylor, artist; Paul Tomidy, independent curator; Karen Tsujimoto, curator, Oakland Museum; Mark Van Proyen, painter and art critic; Tessa Wilcox, art consultant; and Jon Winet, artist.

In the process of assembling the book, I was afforded an excuse to reconnect with old friends I should never have lost touch with in the first place. Many thanks again to Terry Allen, Suzaan Boettger, Vanalyne Green, Rodney Harder, Ann Landi, Judy Malloy, and Yancey Richardson for their generosity and spirit.

My heartfelt thanks to those people who contributed many physical hours to the production of the book: my assistants—Julie Feinstein, Elaine Layton, Veronica Sepe, Sacha Silva, Sarah Steinberg, and the wonderful Dewitt Cheng—who worked tirelessly on every part of the book, and the artists who generously allowed the reproduction of their materials—Jim Banks, Jeanne Herbert, Tom Mallonee, and Alexis White. I also want to thank Leap teachers Jamie Brunson, Jan Camp, and Jil Weinstock for keeping the Leap fires burning while I secluded myself with my computer. And of course, Paul Anchus, for keeping said computer running.

I wish I could take a whole page to sing the praises of the amazing Henni Cohen, who uncomplainingly assumed all my directorial responsibilities in addition to her own, and found time to help edit and even write portions of this book. The information on copyright, resale rights, and legal rights for artists is due entirely to her efforts and expertise; I could not have written the book without her support.

I was luckier than most first-time writers; I was given three editors instead of one. Each of them was endlessly patient, generous of spirit, and turned instantly deaf whenever I started to whine. Thank you

Annie Barrows, Karen Silver, and Jay Schaefer for keeping me working and keeping me laughing. Thanks to editorial assistant Kate Chynoweth for all those educational E-mails, and to copy editor David Featherstone for his painstaking attention to detail and insightful comments. And thank you Jim Paul for instigating the whole thing.

And Oh! My wonderful friends—Joyce Aiken, Sas Colby, Jackie Doumanian, Lori Merish, and Frank Yamrus—not just for helping edit my manuscript without complaint, but for providing unswerving emotional support as I boomeranged my way through the book. Thanks also to Johanna Seppäläinen, my sweet sister Doris Firestein, and my brother-in-law Gordon, for being there when I needed them. Thanks also to my nephew and niece, Aaron and Sondra, for being themselves, and to my mother, Loraine Lang, for her support on every front and her helpful comments about the book itself.

*I*ntroduction

or

How to Tell If You're Really an Artist, and What to Do about It

To be a successful artist, you need three things: curiosity, commitment, and good work habits. You were probably thinking I would say talent.

Talent, according to the prevailing wisdom, is a rare and unpredictable quality usually bestowed upon the lucky recipient at birth. It is commonly believed that if a person is fortunate enough to be born with talent, then everything he or she attempts will be effortless and will astound the world with its brilliance.

It's a compelling idea, but according to reports from certified geniuses like Einstein—who is reported to have said, "Genius is ten percent inspiration, ninety percent perspiration"—it is just a myth. Successful artists in any field will tell you that what appears to other people to be effortless talent is actually the result of single-minded hard work. Of course, people start out with different degrees of ability, but aptitude is only the starting point.

Let's not worry about whether you have talent. Talent is a nonissue. It can be neither measured nor defined, and agonizing over it serves no purpose other than to create both anxiety and, if you've developed a talent for worrying, an excuse for avoiding work.

Each of us, even the least complicated of us, is a vastly complex, endlessly fascinating creature, and the secret to creating art is to gain access to that creature and all that it knows. It is my suspicion that what appears to be talent is really just a doorway to a larger consciousness. As artists, we want to keep the door wide open all the time.

This brings us back to the qualities that *do* lead to success as an artist: curiosity, commitment, and good work habits. Curiosity is vital because an adventurous mind is at the center of all creative endeavors; commitment glues you to the saddle when the ride gets bumpy; and good work habits are necessary because nothing gets done by wishes alone. It's nice to have all three, but I have seen artists do very well with nothing more than meticulously applied work habits.

When I was an undergraduate art student, I was lucky enough to study with internationally acclaimed artist Terry Allen. I loved the class and worshiped the teacher, but I didn't always get my assignments in on time. One day a student asked Terry how you know if you are really an artist. Terry turned to face him and said, "An artist can't stop himself. He really has no choice about it." What an answer! I was mortified. I definitely was not an artist by Terry's definition. Even though I wanted to be an artist more than anything, I wasn't exactly clamoring to be in the studio. To be honest, I spent more time running away from making art than actually making it. Then one evening, after chastising myself for wasting yet another day, I finally understood what Terry meant. What he was really talking about was obsession. It didn't matter whether I was actually making art or not, because if I wasn't making art, I was torturing myself about not making art. *I couldn't stop myself. I didn't have a choice about it.* So my choice wasn't whether or not to be an artist, but whether to be an artist who worked or one who didn't.

Ask yourself this: Am I thinking about making art, or am I thinking about the Super Bowl, world peace, or maybe the laundry? If you find you are rarely thinking about art, then maybe being an artist wasn't your idea in the first place. It is possible you decided to be an artist because your mother noticed that you could draw great pictures of the neighbor's cat. She probably said something along the lines of, "It's a shame to waste your talent." You don't have to draw just because

The first hope of a painter who feels hopeful about painting is the hope that the painting will move, that it will live outside its frame.

GERTRUDE STEIN

you can. You can do lots of things—like read a book, drive a car, hop on one foot—but you don't have to devote your life to them. Release yourself from this obligation and start enjoying the things you really want to do.

I mean it. Put this book down right now and walk away. An artist's life is not an easy one. Do not choose it unless, for you, any other choice would be unthinkable. An artist's career is a roller coaster of incredible highs and unbearable lows (followed by unbearable highs and incredible lows). The art world is fickle; the public will love you one day and ignore you the next. The need to make art will be the one constant in your life as an artist; a deep connection with the art itself is the thing that will sustain you.

Art history is a centuries-long conversation told in pictures. As each new generation enters this conversation, the artists listen to what has been said before, listen to what their inner voices tell them, and then speak, hoping to say something new. It's not easy to find something fresh to say, but what is even more difficult is to know what your own truth is and to speak it regardless of what the art world or anyone else has to say about it. Achieving that kind of authenticity is a tall order, and it is a lifetime job.

Finding your own voice means getting your hands, your eyes, your heart, and your mind in alignment within your work. If, for instance, you've learned to draw very well but you don't have a clue what to draw, then you have your hand and your eye in the work, but you now need to bring your heart and mind to it. If you have lots of great ideas that feel earthshaking in their importance but you don't know how to convey them, then it's time to develop your hand and your eye. This may seem like a simplistic formula, but it can be useful in helping you identify your strengths and weaknesses. If you need to improve your technical skills, find the best teacher you can. If you already have your skills together but you're not sure what you should be doing with them, I suggest keeping a visual diary. A visual diary, a journal of ideas and thoughts about your art, is also known as an artist's notebook. This is a time-honored tradition among artists; almost every important artist you can name kept a visual diary of some kind. It worked for da Vinci; there is no reason it can't work for you. Choose a bound book with unlined pages. It should be large enough

Don't worry about your originality. You couldn't get rid of it even if you wanted to. It will stick with you and show up for better or worse in spite of all you or anyone else can do.

ROBERT HENRI

for making drawings comfortably, and small enough so that you are inclined to carry it with you. Make a habit of working in it daily; sketching ideas and writing down insights.

Here is an exercise for discovering your mission as an artist. Every night before you go to bed, write or sketch three ideas for your art in your journal. Don't make a big production out of this. It doesn't have to take an hour; sometimes five minutes is all you will feel like giving to it. The ideas don't have to be good ones, and you don't ever have to follow through on making them. You just have to imagine them and write them down, or make a sketch if you like. The point is to bring your attention to your work, and to notice the ideas that occur. Within a short time, a week or two, a pattern will begin to emerge. As you browse through your journal, you will notice that some of your ideas aren't so bad, some are truly stupid, and some actually seem deep and important. Pay close attention to these ideas. This is your heart speaking. It is telling you where your work wants to go. Once you begin working on a project, continue keeping the diary; the work will become clearer daily.

One's mind, once stretched by a new idea, never regains its original dimension.
OLIVER WENDELL HOLMES, SR.

Knowing when you are ready to start exhibiting your art is one of the most bewildering issues an artist has to face. One problem is that we are led astray by our egos. Your ego will tell you what a genius you are and that the world needs your profound insights, and two minutes later it will turn around and announce that you are too stupid to live. I have been making art for over fifteen years, and my ego still does this to me regularly. It is not uncommon for me to wake up in the morning, take a look at yesterday's work, and be overcome by my own blazing brilliance, only to replace that warm feeling with the deepest despair at the end of the day.

When it comes to putting your work out in the world, you will need a more reliable way to measure when you are ready. One way to gain a wider vision is to show it to someone you respect and ask for their feedback. Likely candidates for this are art teachers and artists who are knowledgeable and accomplished in your area of art. If this is the first time you are showing your work to anyone, you will probably be feeling a little apprehensive about asking for feedback. Think carefully about who you choose to ask, and show the work to several people, not just one. Don't put yourself in the position of allowing one person's opinion to carry too much weight. We have all heard stories about important artists whose teachers told them they would be better off planting radishes. Thankfully, those artists ignored that advice. Remember that, in asking for feedback, you are gathering responses to help you understand the impact of your art, that is all. Ultimately your opinion is the one that counts most.

Another way to judge how your work will fit into the marketplace is to frequent art galleries and museums. The exhibitions at contemporary art galleries change every month or two. Not only will you get to see some terrific art, but you will soon get a feel for what is being shown and sold. If you live in a major city, make a habit of seeing these shows regularly. If you don't live in a major city, make special plans to visit one; it will be well worth the effort.

Art is either plagiarism or revolution.

PAUL GAUGUIN

Some artists complete three paintings and start exhibiting right away. I think this is a mistake. You need time to develop your craft. You need time to find your voice. These things should occur in the privacy of your studio, not in the public forum. If the art world is confronted with underdeveloped work, it won't be interested in returning for a second look. Also, it is necessary for an artist to be free from public response, both good and bad, while the artwork is still in its formative stage. It is easy to ruin a promising body of work by exposing it to public scrutiny; you will either gain so much praise you won't need to finish the work, or so much criticism you won't feel you can.

In order to market your art, you need a body of work to market. A body of work is a series of pieces that holds together in some way, that seems to have something in common. Usually each piece employs the same medium, like oil paint, but a body of work must be more specific than that. The art must be united thematically or stylistically, and usually both. A body of work can't just be the same painting repeated with minor variations, it should show an in-depth exploration of a single idea, or related ideas. It should engage the viewer in that exploration, and each piece in the series should expand the viewer's understanding of the ideas the artist is pursuing.

Once you have found your voice and developed a cohesive body of work, in order to establish a career as a successful visual artist, you must have a clear understanding of how the art world works—who the important people are, what their background is likely to be, what their prejudices are, what their day is like, where their skills and interests lie, what their bottom line is, which institutions and galleries are available to artists, how to approach them, and on and on. If you don't want to take the time to learn all this information about the marketplace, you will need to hire someone who does. Or you can be like Blanche DuBois and rely on the kindness of strangers. Hers was actually not a bad plan for artists of former generations, when the world was a kinder, slower place and there were fewer artists. Today, the art world is still experiencing the aftershock of the excesses and expectations of the 1980s; the waters are in turmoil, castles are tumbling, and there are still quite a few sharks near the shores. As an artist, you need to know what to expect and how to deal with it.

This book is designed for use by artists at all levels of their careers: artists just getting out of school ready to fast-forward to success and fame; midcareer artists who want to accelerate the progression of their careers; and once-active artists returning to the art world after an absence. Each category of artist will want to use the book in a different way.

If you are entering the art world for the first time, or if you are returning after a prolonged absence, read the chapters in sequence. Beginners should read them in sequence because they won't want to miss any of the information; returnees because the art world has changed a lot in the last few years. The organization of the chapters is designed to follow a natural progression of activities, each chapter building on the last. Reading the chapters in order will provide a fundamental understanding of the world you will be entering, as well as demonstrate the activities you will be undertaking, in an organized and easy-to-follow manner.

If you are a seasoned artist, use your intuition about which parts are appropriate for you. You already know some of the information, and other ideas will be quite new to you. Chapter one might be a good place to start, since it examines a wider range of exhibition possibilities than is normally associated with the art world; then maybe chapter four, which discusses career strategies in detail. Once you have your plan in mind, look at the earlier chapters to fine-tune your promotional materials. Chapter two will professionalize your artist's packet, and chapter three is good for helping you focus on your

The creative habit is like a drug. The particular obsession changes, but the excitement, the thrill of your creation lasts.

HENRY MOORE

choices. Chapter five discusses gallery relationships and negotiations; chapter six provides tips for organizing your workspace and streamlining tasks. In chapter seven, you will find step-by-step directions for every aspect of staging your own exhibition, and in chapter eight secrets to effective networking. Take a look at chapter nine, as well, since it addresses problems specific to the midcareer artist.

The big secret for all readers is to *use* the information as you learn it. Maybe you can't act on everything immediately (unless you have unlimited time, a trust fund, and an office of secretaries at your disposal), but make a point of starting to integrate some of what you are learning into the way you live now. Don't wait until you win the jackpot; you may be waiting a long time. Start living your life as an artist now. All big goals begin with little steps. And don't forget, choosing to be an artist is a good and generous act. The world needs its artists, whether it knows it or not.

Art happens—no hovel is safe from it, no prince may depend upon it, the vastest intelligence cannot bring it about.

JAMES McNEILL
WHISTLER

CHAPTER ONE

A World of Possibilities

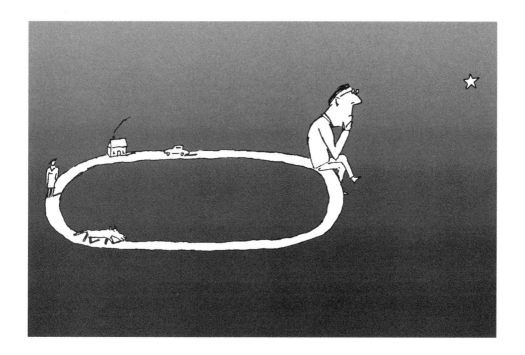

In the art world, the hottest issue today is guaranteed to be old news by next week. Art may be eternal, but the attention span of the art world is roughly the blink of an eye. In your lifetime as an artist, you will see dozens of art movements come and go, hundreds of galleries spring up and disappear, and governments at all levels alter their policies regarding the arts. Entire mechanisms for support of the arts will collapse and then be replaced by something new, and painting will be declared dead at least once every five years. If you take all of this as a given, riding the ups and downs of your career will feel like an unfolding adventure rather than a series of unexpected jolts.

What doesn't change, however, is the impulse to create. Artists will always make art; we can't help ourselves. Imagination is inherent in the human species. This ability to wonder "what if?" is what makes us different from the rest of the animals on the planet. Blessed with a creative intelligence, and our amazing opposable thumb, human beings were born to be artists.

In Europe, prior to the mid–eighteenth century, artists made their living by fulfilling commissions for the church or the king. There was no great division between the kind of art they created as work and what they did as art. Today, there are no great patrons existing to support the arts on such a scale. This lack of support brings with it a lack of external control. With the end of the patronage system, artists began to turn their attention to subjects other than the glorification of the king or the church.

The concept of art-for-art's-sake is fairly new. This is what the art critic Thomas Crow calls "freely conceived art" and what contemporary critic Bill Berkson christened "art that nobody asked for." Art today can be seen as a response to both the breakdown of the royal and clerical patronage system and the democratization of Western culture. Over the past two centuries, artists began to make art on their own cognizance; nobody was supplying them with subject matter. At the same time, salons began to be organized to exhibit this new work to the general public and art became available to the shopkeeper as well as the aristocrat.

No one knew what to make of an art that was no longer defined by the exterior restrictions of religion and class. How did one know if the art was any good, or even what it was about? Hence the birth of the art critic (an expert to help people figure out what to think), the gallery system (with its experts to help people spend their money), and the art market (all those experts who participate in the buying and selling of art).

Over the years the gallery system has become the principle means by which artists reach the public. Traditionally the gallery system has worked this way: The artist labors in a garret and, at some point, if lucky and talented, is discovered by a gallery. The artwork is then consigned to the gallery to be displayed and sold. (Notice that the work is *consigned* to the gallery, not sold to it—an important distinc-

If I didn't start painting, I would have raised chickens.

GRANDMA MOSES

tion indicating that the gallery, not the artist, is setting the rules here.) If the work is purchased, the artist receives a percentage of the selling price; if it isn't, the gallery holds it for a while and eventually either sells it or returns it to the artist.

This doesn't sound like a terrific deal for the artists, and certainly no other kind of manufacturer would consent to so one-sided an arrangement; but artists do not define themselves as manufacturers. They are seekers on a quest. As any hopeful before the divine, an artist only wishes to be found worthy (and, one hopes, to gain wealth and fame in the bargain). Acceptance by a gallery conveys worth and brings the art to the attention of critics and collectors. Since the gallery makes all the career decisions, the artist is free to do what he or she wants to do most, make art. The problem with the gallery system is that it is modeled on a parent-child relationship, with the artist (as child) relinquishing control over personal affairs to the gallery. If the gallery is a wise, affectionate, and savvy parent, this arrangement can be beneficial for both parties. But how many of us feel our parents did a perfect job? And, more to the point, why should a stranger be any better?

The true work of art is but a shadow of the divine perfection.
MICHELANGELO

The traditional gallery system does have its attractions, however. Let us say you were accepted by the perfect gallery in the 1960s; what could you expect? You could expect the gallery to mount a yearly solo exhibition of your work, handle all the advertising and publicity for your show, and constantly court the art critics, museum curators, and especially the art collectors. The gallery would arrange for the framing and hanging of the show. It would negotiate with clients to get the best prices for your work. Between shows, it would keep your art on hand and unfurl it proudly for prospective collectors throughout the year. It would secure the payment from your sales, subtract a percentage as commission (it used to be as low as 10 percent in Van Gogh's day, but has been increasing steadily over the years so that now the standard is 50 percent), and promptly deliver the rest to you. If you were experiencing hard times, the gallery would remain steadfastly by your side. It would advance you money when you needed it and say "there there" when you were having trouble sleeping.

Leo Castelli was the epitome of this kind of dealer. Stories abound of his generosity and support for the artists he represented. If he mounted a show of an artist's new work and nothing sold, he would either buy the art himself or advance the artist money against future sales because he *believed* in the value of the work. Castelli was in it for the long term, and most of the artists he represented—Jasper Johns, Robert Rauschenberg, and Roy Lichtenstein, to name a few—have become household names.

Examples such as this are wonderful, but they have filled today's artists with unrealistic expectations when they search for a gallery to handle their own art. Times have changed. The yearly solo show is a thing of the past, and shows are now scheduled two to three years in advance. Galleries still arrange the publicity for their exhibitions (design and print announcements, write press releases, contact critics), but increasingly they are asking the artist to share in these costs. In the current economy it has become common practice for galleries to offer discounts to important collectors, art consultants, and other dealers and museums (usually around 20 percent). In the past, the gallery absorbed these costs, now they ask the artist to share them. Framing the art is now often the artist's responsibility, as are all or part of the shipping costs. The gallery staff labors enthusiastically for the artist while the exhibition is installed, but once it is down, most of their energy is occupied by the next artist's show. Although the standard gallery-artist split has been fifty-fifty for quite a while, I have recently begun hearing rumors of galleries asking for sixty-forty, in their favor. In fairness to the galleries, the recent recession in the early 1990s has been very difficult for them. The galleries who survived did so by tightening their belts, giving discounts on artwork, decreasing their staff, and increasing their artist base.

Today's artists tend to look at the opulence of the 1980s and think of it as the norm, but most seasoned art professionals describe that time as an aberration. Many speak of it wistfully, but I tend to agree with one New York art dealer's assessment of the experience: Before the 1980s, the art world had been proceeding as it had for a century or so, with artists making art, critics discussing it, curators looking for the historical links, and galleries selling it to a small group of people who cared passionately about being a part of it all. Some artists and galleries did well, others didn't; no one became outrageously rich, but everyone was in it for the love of art and there was a balance to the

I don't believe in art.
I believe in artists.
MARCEL DUCHAMP

whole mechanism. Then art became fashionable, and suddenly every-one with money to play with and an eye for a quick buck started buying art. Prices soared. Auction houses astounded everyone by commanding higher and higher prices with every sale. Contemporary art was selling almost as fast as it was made, and no price seemed too high. International magazines and newspapers reported record sales daily, and more new art lovers joined the fray. Universities expanded their art departments, and enrollment multiplied.

Then the economy collapsed, the entire country went into a reces-sion, and artists were left with art that no one would buy. The art was priced too high, and everyone was reducing spending; besides, col-lecting art was no longer the coolest thing to do. The art schools, how-ever, continued to pour out hopeful young artists, many of them filled with expectations of wealth and fame, but now there was no longer a system in balance to support them. There were too many artists, not enough galleries, and not enough collectors.

I don't have to tell you that the art market looked pretty bleak as it headed into the 1990s. Many galleries could no longer afford the high rents they had been paying. At the height of the recession, an article in the *New York Times* reported at one point that as many as thirty art gal-leries a month were closing in New York City alone. This seems an ex-aggeration, but there is no doubt that the face of the art world was changing dramatically.

But that time, too, has passed. New galleries and fresh forms of ex-hibition spaces are emerging across the country. These galleries tend to be characterized by smaller budgets, less prestigious locations, less expensive art, and youthful, energetic proprietors who have an in-creased willingness to do whatever it takes to create a space that wel-comes and engages the art-viewing public.

As an artist, you will need to make decisions about whether or not to pursue representation by a commercial gallery. The answer will be based on your ultimate goals. If you are determined to make it in the Big Time—that is, to gain international recognition for making a significant contribution to art history and to have your art sold to important museum and private collectors—then eventually you will need to enter the gallery system. There is no doubt that represen-tation by a respected gallery significantly adds to an artist's status. In

It is not clear that intelligence has any long-term survival value.
STEPHEN HAWKING

addition, the gallery often has access to influential collectors and art professionals who are difficult for an artist to reach alone. But each gallery approaches these things differently, with varying levels of expertise and commitment; it is not uncommon for a gallery to take on a new artist, put out a little effort, and eventually consign the work to a drawer in the back room, where it is occasionally pulled out to show to clients. At that point, the only advantage of being in the gallery is for the status, a dubious advantage at best.

If your goals as an artist place more emphasis on sales than on recognition, then representation by a gallery is only one of the ways of achieving this. You can also sell your work through art consultants, poster and greeting-card companies, open studios, and even mail order. If your finished artwork takes a more conceptual, less concretely physical form, then hunting for a commercial gallery to represent you will be a fruitless exercise, at least at the beginning of your career. Commercial galleries will not consider handling art unless they can see a way to make money from it.

To help you decide how best to have your work seen by the public, it might be useful to look at the structure of the art world to learn how the pieces fit together and understand how each part functions.

All art has this characteristic: It unites people.

LEO TOLSTOY

The Exhibition Spaces

Established exhibition spaces fall into six categories: museums, non-profit galleries, alternative spaces, commercial galleries, university galleries, and artist co-ops. I have also added a seventh category, called *nontraditional venues,* which is a catch-all for everything else. Each type of exhibition space has a different focus, although there is often some overlapping of functions.

Museums. As keepers of culture that collect and preserve art and hold it in trust for future generations, museums perceive their role in the art world to be historical. The names of many museums reflect a specific focus, like the Museum of Modern Art or the Jewish Museum. Since the emphasis of a museum is on art history, it will generally be reluctant to show work by emerging artists. In order to obtain a show

Art World Ladder of Success

Type of Exhibition Space	Status Indicators	Publicity Indicators
World Class Museums		Favorable Review in the *New York Times*
High Profile New York Galleries	Shiny Floors, Art Hung Sparsely, Stylish Staff	Not So Good Review in the *New York Times*
National Museums		
High Profile Galleries Not in New York		Feature Article in a Glossy Art Magazine
High Profile Alternative Spaces		Reviews in Glossy Art Magazines
Medium to Small Museums		Reviews in National Newspapers
Most Commercial Galleries	White Walls, Art Installed Carefully	Reviews in Regional Art Magazines
University Galleries		Reviews in Local Newspapers
Low Profile Galleries	Boutique Atmosphere, Many Kinds of Art, Haphazardly Displayed	
Restaurants, Hotels, Retail Stores, Cafés, Beauty Parlors	Primary Activity is Eating or Grooming	Calendar Listings in Local Newspapers
Your Home	Work Hung in Bathroom	Your Roommate Likes It

in a museum, it is necessary to gain a reputation for your art first through another venue, such as a commercial or nonprofit gallery, or a media-attracting public event. Museums are dependent upon memberships, grants, and major donors for their financial support. Museums do not sell art, except through adjunct galleries that are usually organized as art rental galleries. Museum rental galleries exhibit art by local artists rather than work from their permanent collections.

Nonprofit galleries. Nonprofit art galleries are similar to museums, but they tend to be smaller and lack permanent collections. Instead of an historical focus, they usually emphasize contemporary art. Like museums, they are supported by memberships and grants. There are several kinds of nonprofit spaces: municipal nonprofit spaces, nonprofit spaces focused around a specific medium or issue, and alternative spaces.

Municipal nonprofit spaces are usually created under the auspices of a city or county government. They may be run by city employees and be funded directly by the city, or they may be administered by an adjunct group that raises the funds for the gallery by using the city's nonprofit status as an umbrella. Most American towns and cities have at least one municipal nonprofit gallery. You can usually recognize them by the words *Art Center* or *Cultural Center* associated with the name of a city, as in the Berkeley Art Center and the Chicago Cultural Center. These galleries tend to focus on art by local artists, which makes them ideal candidates for emerging artists. Because a government organization is involved, municipal galleries tend to favor artwork that does not disturb the status quo.

Issue-focused and medium-specific spaces are created by groups of people with an interest in a specific kind of art. The International Center for Photography and the Drawing Center, both in New York City, and the Photographic Resource Center in Boston are examples of galleries established around a specific medium. Examples of issue-oriented spaces are The Sacred Circle Gallery in Seattle, which exhibits Native American art; the Art Research Center in Kansas City, which focuses on art and science; and the Yerba Buena Center in San Francisco, which emphasizes cultural diversity.

The universe is full of magical things patiently waiting for our wits to grow sharper.

EDEN PHILLPOTTS

Alternative spaces. Alternative art spaces tend to show work that is on the cutting edge. This type of gallery first appeared in the art world in the 1970s, during the heyday of performance art, conceptual art, and mail art—all the art forms that are now called *new genres*. Artists were fed up with the commercial emphasis of the art world. They wanted a place to show experimental art that wasn't influenced by its ability to sell, so they rented buildings and inaugurated their own galleries. Many of the early alternative spaces have not survived into the nineties, but an amazing number of the best ones are still with us, and new ones are being born daily. Today's alternative art space is usually an artist-run nonprofit space with a small staff and most of the work performed by passionate volunteers. Budgets for alternative spaces are usually small. If your art falls into the new genre category, alternative spaces are perfect for you; if you happen to be a traditional painter, probably not. Things move slowly at alternative spaces. Exhibition schedules are often decided by committee, and the staff is always overworked and underpaid, so be patient. Shows change regularly and are usually accompanied by announcements and receptions, just like uptown. Some of the better-known alternative spaces include the Clocktower and the Kitchen in New York, LACE (Los Angeles Contemporary Exhibitions) in Los Angeles, The Capp Street Project in San Francisco, and N.A.M.E. in Chicago.

Commercial art galleries. The business of selling art falls to commercial galleries. They bring the latest art-world discoveries to the people who will buy them, mostly the wealthy. This means they must maintain a look of wealth themselves. To hang the art, they have to rent large spaces in high-rent neighborhoods, then decorate and maintain those spaces to pristine perfection. Most gallery owners do not have art history backgrounds, just a love of art. Many of them once planned to be artists, but got sidetracked along the way. Quite a few of the most successful gallery owners come from wealthy backgrounds; this gives them access to the right people, which is good for the artists who are with them. Sometimes running the gallery is just a hobby, which is not so good for the artists. If a gallery owner isn't rolling in money he or she is going to have to work very hard to succeed.

Many a man fails as an original thinker simply because his memory is too good.

FRIEDRICH NIETZSCHE

When a commercial gallery considers an artist's work, money is always the bottom line. The expenses are just too high for an owner to behave otherwise. That is not to say that galleries don't occasionally take work they know will be difficult to sell. They do, but they have to balance it carefully with more accessible work in order to keep the doors open.

When investigating galleries to handle your work, bear in mind that galleries are as individual as the people who own them. Each gallery has a specific focus. Determine what it is before you contact them. If you are not sure how to do this, examine chapter four for some pointers. Don't waste your time bringing feathered jewelry to a gallery that handles only vintage photographs. Edith Caldwell, who owns a contemporary realism gallery in San Francisco, reports that every day she receives slides from artists whose work holds no relationship to the realistic paintings her gallery is known for. Not only does this waste a gallery director's time, it tends to put him or her in a bad mood for the next artist who comes along.

Commercial galleries vary widely in terms of status in the art world. You can usually discern the status of a gallery the moment you walk in, even without looking at the art. In general, the whiter and emptier the walls, and the shinier the floors, the more "important" the gallery is. To make it easier to recognize the kind of gallery you are in, I have divided contemporary art galleries into four distinct groups: the New York model, young and hot, boutique-style, and the disreputable gallery.

The New York model is the one I described above. The walls are white and freshly painted; the floor shines. It holds mostly one-person shows, and the exhibits change every month. The gallery designs and prints announcements for each new show and hosts an opening reception. The high-profile galleries get reviewed in the newspaper. Check out the outfits of the gallery staff. Do their clothes look expensive, with just a touch of insouciance? You are probably in a New York–style gallery.

Young and hot galleries follow the style of the New York model, but with a smaller budget. The director and the artists are usually newly out of art school, and they make up for limited funds with a nonchalant attitude and imaginative events. Exhibits change monthly, the gallery space is usually in a trendy but dilapidated part of town, and they often get reviewed. If your work fits into this category (and you fit into the twenty-something age bracket), hooking up with a young and hot gallery could be just the right thing for your career. You and the gallery can ascend the success ladder together.

Boutique-style galleries can be recognized by a wide range of artistic styles and mediums packed into one space. In a boutique-style gallery, it is not unusual to see watercolor paintings by one artist displayed next to oil paintings by another, with a jewelry display case next to a ceramic sculpture. There are no regularly changing exhibitions here; the gallery director will hang a piece for a while and change it when the spirit moves. They hold no receptions and rarely get reviewed. Showing your work in this kind of gallery is not going to help you become famous, but you may sell some work.

Disreputable galleries are the ones to watch out for. They are often located in high-traffic tourist districts, such as Fisherman's Wharf in San Francisco. Not all galleries in tourist areas fall into this category, but a tourist area is a perfect location for a disreputable gallery because most of the people who walk in don't have any knowledge of contemporary art. These galleries snag unwary customers by promising them that the work they are buying is an investment that has surged in value. Often, the real reason the value of the work has increased is because after selling the first piece by that artist, the gallery has doubled the price on the second. The gallery operators trap unwary artists into signing ironclad contracts that basically put the artists into a type of forced servitude. I have heard of contracts that not only require an artist to complete a certain number of paintings a week, but dictate subject matter and style. A gallery contract can be a good thing (we will talk about them in another chapter), but never sign one without careful scrutiny. If possible show it to a lawyer. If you don't have access to a lawyer, check out the appendix in this book for some leads, or call your state art council.

> *The reasonable man adapts himself to the world; the unreasonable one persists in trying to adapt the world to himself. Therefore all progress depends on the unreasonable man.*
>
> GEORGE BERNARD SHAW

University galleries. There are often several different kinds of gallery spaces on university and college campuses, and they are wonderful places for emerging artists to show their work. The big universities usually have a museum (which is commonly reserved for showing established artists), but there is often gallery space available in the art department, the design department, or the student union, and sometimes in campus hallways. At least one of these spaces may be available for off-campus artists. The shows are often curated by a teacher, who is willing to look at work by lesser-known artists. Although these shows rarely have receptions or announcements, they do carry the prestige of the university, which is a nice thing to add to your résumé. If you have a show at a university, your work will be seen by hundreds of students; while they often make an attentive and inquisitive audience, you probably won't sell any work.

Artist co-ops. Artist co-ops are the art world's equivalent of the literary world's vanity press. They flourished in the 1970s, the same time as alternative spaces. A group of artists would get together, find a space, share the cost of the rent and the work duties and, in exchange, each artist would get a yearly show. This is a great way to gain hands-on experience in running a gallery, and if you're the kind of artist who works best with a deadline looming ahead of you, co-ops are good for helping you get some work done. You will meet some nice people, but don't expect the co-op to assist your career much. Since everyone knows the artists pay to exhibit there, the shows usually are not reviewed. Each co-op is organized a little differently, but the ones that set aside a part of their gallery space for nonmember shows tend to be taken more seriously. If you live in a city with an active art community, consider other exhibition options first; but if you reside in a small town, a co-op gallery can help create fellowship among artists and establish a support system for art.

Nontraditional venues. This is the term I use for anything that doesn't fit into the categories listed above. A nontraditional venue can be any place that isn't customarily considered an exhibition space, such as a restaurant, a bank, a one-night gallery, a hotel room, a corporate building, a storefront window, a coffee shop, a hospital, a hair salon, a night club, a shopping bag, a shopping cart, a Web site, or a public-access television show. The possibilities are as endless as your imagination. Creating or discovering a new place to show art is a great way to be involved in your community. Art shown in a café is art that is participating in the culture, rather than being isolated from it. This adds vitality to the community. The disadvantage is that there is no gallery staff to attend to details like opening receptions, show announcements, press releases, and sales. You will have to take responsibility for those things yourself. The advantage is that you gain control over those elements; and if the event is conducted with panache, you may attract more public attention than you would with an ordinary gallery show.

Who the Players Are

The artist. That's you. I don't need to say much about the artist except to remind you that, as the artist, *you are central* to the whole mechanism. Without the artist, there is no art world.

The curator. An art curator may work at a museum, nonprofit gallery, or alternative art space, or have a freelance career. The curator's job is to recognize trends in art-making and create themes for exhibitions based on what they see and think. Curators select the work, oversee the hanging of the show, and write about the work for a catalog, if there is one. They are often expected to raise the money for the show, as well. They are paid by the institution for which they work.

Curators at museums usually have a background in art history; the more prestigious the museum, the more extensive the curator's art history credentials will be. They work long hours for amazingly low pay. It is not unusual for a curator to devote well over forty hours a week overseeing installation of shows, writing catalogs, applying for grants, maintaining a permanent collection, and going to committee meetings. On top of all their other duties, they are expected to attend evening social functions such as exhibition receptions and fund-raising dinners, sometimes several times a week. Most of the curators

I have met care passionately about art. When they look at art, it is from the point of view of art history, and the questions and issues they raise will reflect that. When they look at art by lesser known artists, they are doing so to acquaint themselves with new work being done in their area in order to generate new ideas for shows. They are not interested in what they call derivative art—art that mimics another artist's work. From the point of view of art history, there is already one Matisse; we don't need thirty more. Curators will be most interested in art that breaks boundaries or that makes them see things in a new way.

Curators for nonprofit and alternative art spaces work just as hard and get paid even less. Often they are artists themselves, juggling creator and curatorial careers at the same time. Since the curatorial focus at nonprofit spaces is usually on contemporary art, rather than its historical precedents, these curators will be interested in a wider range of work. They still have to stay within the defined focus of their gallery, however, so determine that your art fits before approaching them.

The art dealer. The role of the art dealer is to sell artwork, so the art dealer can usually be found in a commercial art gallery, although some private dealers do not maintain a public space. Sometimes the terms *dealer* and *gallery* are used interchangeably. It is the dealer's job to do whatever is possible to advance the artist's career so that the value of the work continues to grow. Dealers, who usually represent fifteen to thirty artists, spend a lot of time on the phone trying to bring in curators, collectors, and critics to see the work they carry. They plan career strategies, store artwork, and arrange exhibitions. In exchange, they usually expect exclusive rights to the sale of your art within their immediate geographic area. Beware of any dealer who asks for worldwide rights unless that dealer has unusually extensive art-world connections. Even then, I'd think twice. How can one dealer be everywhere at once? Sometimes, in a large city like New York, an artist will have two galleries, one uptown and one downtown. This arrangement should be done with the full knowledge and agreement of all parties concerned. Art dealers are fond of calling the artist-dealer relationship a marriage, which basically means they need to feel they can trust you to treat them fairly and honestly. You should expect the

An art school is a place where about three people work with feverish energy and everybody else idles to a degree that I should have conceived unattainable by human nature.

G. K. CHESTERTON

same in return. The standard financial artist-dealer relationship is fifty-fifty on any sales made by the gallery.

The art consultant. The art consultant does not belong to a gallery. He or she is hired by a collector or a corporation to help them acquire a collection of art. The difference between an art consultant and an art dealer is that while an art dealer shepherds the careers of a number of artists, art consultants have no such allegiances. Their job is to oversee the creation of an art collection based on the client's interests and needs. For instance, the client may be a trucking company with an urge to fill all twenty-three offices with pictures of trucks. The art consultant's job is to find a selection of images of trucks for the client to choose from. The art consultant rarely keeps inventory in stock, but likes to have a varied collection of slides on hand. Art consultants don't maintain a gallery space and expect no exclusive rights. They generally are paid a fee by the client, but also expect a discount from the artist, anywhere from 20 to 40 percent. If they buy work through an art dealer, they will expect the dealer to give them a discount (usually 20 percent), which the dealer may or may not require the artist to share.

> *The annual output of all American art schools is probably around 35,000 graduates.*
>
> ROBERT HUGHES

When you send your slides to an art consultant, don't expect an immediate response. Sometimes the slides are kept up to a year before anything happens. Then again, you might receive a phone call within a week announcing ten pieces had just sold. This used to happen more often in the eighties, when the economy was booming; but working with a good art consultant is still a great way to sell art. Since art consultants sell mainly to corporations and the work is hung in public buildings such as hospitals, hotels, and corporate work spaces, they will be looking for art that doesn't offend anyone. If you are making paintings of copulating crayfish, the art consultant is not for you.

The agent. I get at least one phone call a week from some young artist asking if I can recommend a good agent. Unfortunately, I never can. There are lots of agents in the commercial art world, as in the literary world, but not in the fine art world. That is probably because art dealers have traditionally done the work of an agent, which is to manage the artist's career. With the decrease in responsibility on the part of the galleries, the idea of an agent has become more and more attractive to artists. There is obviously a need. But a problem arises with how they are to be paid. Some agents want to be paid a set monthly fee by the artist; while this makes sense for the agent, most artists don't have the money to pay them. Others try a percentage system (say 15 percent, like literary agents) but the problem is that almost everyone else in the art world—like galleries and art consultants—expects a percentage as well, and they are not always happy to share. Most agents I know end up becoming private dealers or move on to some other role in the art world. The one or two successful artist agents I have known were already well connected in the art world and were careful to take on only a handful of well-established artists.

The art collector. There can never be enough of the rare breed known as the art collector. Although the stereotype is the wealthy socialite, anyone can become a collector. All one really needs is a love of art. Vance Martin, a private art dealer in San Francisco, once told me that his real job is to be an educator, to help collectors develop their eye. A new collector will come to him wanting to buy a piece by some well-known artist, such as Ansel Adams. The dealer will help the collector buy the piece, and then he will show him other work, work by artists who may not be so obviously in the public eye. The more the collector sees and has a chance to talk about art, the more sophisticated his way of seeing becomes. He eventually ends up with a collection that is uniquely his own.

Your first collectors will be your family and friends. Don't shy away from this; every artist started this way. See it as a first step on your way to a healthy career. When a friend asks to buy a piece of your art, your first impulse will probably be to say, "Oh no. Here, I'll just give it to you." Fight that impulse. If your friends want to buy your work, let them. They want to show their support for you. They want to be part of it all. In years to come, they can say they "knew you when" and brag about how much more the work is worth today.

The critic. Every art critic I have ever met has held a definite opinion about the role of art criticism. No two definitions have ever been alike. I have come to the conclusion that the job of an art critic is to have an

Art is a plaything for the idle rich. So are artists.
DAVE HICKEY

Criticism is prejudice made plausible.
H. L. MENCKEN

opinion. It is better if it is an informed opinion, but this gets confusing since all of them believe that theirs *is* an informed opinion. Since there is no way to measure this, and really no criteria for becoming a critic, the question becomes moot. All it takes to become a critic is to write a review that someone is willing to print, which is surprisingly easy. Some critics have art history backgrounds, some have writing backgrounds, and many of them are also artists. Most express a very definite set of ethics (such as a taboo against writing reviews of their friends' work, or accepting gifts from artists) but, as with everything, the definitions of what is ethical vary widely. Critics get paid almost nothing for their work, so, just like artists, most of them hold a second job as well. It takes a lot of courage to be an art critic and to put yourself on the line in print, particularly since the rewards are dubious. If you are outspoken you tend to make enemies, and the friendships you make among artists are always suspect. On the other hand, you tend to get invited to all the best parties.

No statue has ever been put up to a critic.
JEAN SIBELIUS

How the Art World Is Changing

When the art market crashed in the early nineties, galleries folded, collectors started selling off their collections, art dealers started looking for second jobs, and the commercial art scene looked very bleak. If supporting the arts was fashionable in the eighties, withdrawing that support became fashionable in the nineties, especially in Congress. It wasn't long before the National Endowment for the Arts was on death row, and thousands of vital nonprofit and alternative art spaces were propelled to the brink of extinction.

I have forced myself to contradict myself in order to avoid conforming to my own taste.
MARCEL DUCHAMP

Everybody began searching for new ways to survive. It wasn't easy, there was a lot of grumbling, and some didn't make it. But now several years have passed; the American economy itself is on the rise, and everywhere I hear tales of new growth. Museum membership is growing again, and New York art dealers are reporting a record increase in new collectors for 1997. I think we can safely say the dust has settled.

This shake-up of the established art marketing system has opened possibilities for working outside the system. In virtually every city, new venues for showing work are appearing. The art world of the eighties may have been about money and the moneyed classes, but in the nineties it is about ingenuity and reaching a wider, more diverse audience. This means there is room for a more diverse art.

Think of the whole world, real and virtual, as your gallery space, and start from there. There are many more ways of being an artist than just sitting back and waiting for some gallery to welcome you onto its hallowed walls. Not only is it exciting to be taking your career into your own hands, but it often turns out to be an effective strategy. Innovation is a great way to attract the attention of the art world. Why not let it come to you.

Some Examples of People Who Found Creative Ways to Exist as Artists

Reverend Howard Finster. Reverend Finster started painting at the age of sixty. He was in the process of repairing and painting a bicycle when he spied a face in a smudge of paint on the tip of his finger and heard the voice of God. God spoke unto him: "Paint five thousand sacred works of art." So he did. His paintings are bright and fresh and filled with words, and when he finishes a painting he paints the can the paint came in, the rag he wiped the canvas with, and anything else in sight. Originally Finster just wanted to decorate his little garden (which he calls "Paradise Garden" and the *Washington Post* called "God's Little Junkyard") with the word of God, but the word has spread. The garden now covers three acres and includes elaborately painted buildings, trees, and objects, as well as a gift shop run by his family. "I'm not out trying to make money or to be a big artist. I'm trying to get the world straightened out." The wonderful part is that, in the process, he has become a big artist, and his works are in demand at top galleries and museums around the world.

The Guerrilla Girls. As the self-proclaimed "Conscience of the Art World," the Guerrilla Girls is a band of anonymous artists fighting for the elimination of sexism and racism in the art community. Established in the mid-eighties in response to the shocking lack of women in the Museum of Modern Art's blockbuster exhibit *International Survey of Contemporary Painting and Sculpture,* the Guerrilla Girls decided

Genius is the capacity for productive reaction against one's training.

BERNARD BERENSON

If God gives you a vision, get with it. God knows what people want.

REVEREND HOWARD FINSTER

to fight back by plastering New York with posters that pointed out the statistical discrepancies. The posters were savvy, sarcastic, and compelling. They named names and printed statistics with their sources, so they could not be easily dismissed. The posters have become such collector's items that new "releases" don't remain on the walls very long. The members maintain their anonymity by appearing in public wearing gorilla masks with miniskirts and high heels. Their mailing address is a post office box, and their phone is answered by a mechanized answering machine. They feel anonymity is important for keeping attention focused on the issues, instead of on personalities. This serves to make them even more intriguing to the media. Through their efforts they keep important cultural issues alive and have a lot of fun doing it. They have appeared at symposia, on television, and in glossy magazines. They now sell their posters in signed editions, each of which is stamped with their signature banana and sealed with a lipstick kiss. The money goes to support their nonprofit foundation.

Nobody can be exactly like me. Even I have trouble doing it.
TALLULAH BANKHEAD

The Art-o-mat. Dubbed by the *Wall Street Journal* as the world's first coin-operated art gallery, the Art-o-mat is really just a storefront in Portland, Oregon, where artist Stephanie Porter has created her irreverent kinetic installations. By slipping a quarter into a slot, the viewer can activate the voice of Dr. Niketime, the all-night psychic, or get baptized into the Church of Elvis. According to Stephanie, during her best month she made $750 in quarters.

When I first heard about the Art-o-mat, I envisioned a storefront with curtains that could be opened by inserting a coin as a showcase for changing exhibitions. That is not the way Stephanie used her idea, however; at the Art-o-mat, the insertion of a quarter activates different parts of the exhibit. I still think the curtain idea could have dramatic possibilities, so I am throwing it out here. After all, everyone always wants to know what is behind a curtain.

J. S. G. Boggs. J. S. G. Boggs is an artist who literally makes money. He draws detailed renderings of currency from around the world in color, one side only, but changes minute details to phrases like "The Bank of Boggs" or "J. S. G. Boggs, Secretary of the Measury." Boggs refuses to sell his art; he will only spend it. When he dines at a restaurant, he offers to pay for the meal with one of his creations, making it clear to the waiter that he made it himself, that he is offering to pay with art, not money. If the waiter accepts it as equal to money, Boggs expects change in return. If the check was $17.50 and he gave the waiter a twenty dollar Boggs's Bill, he will expect to receive $2.50 in change. An interesting conversation then ensues, usually involving the manager at some point, and eventually they come to an agreement. A surprising number of people accept his proposal. Boggs says the ratio is about one in ten. When he has completed a successful transaction, he saves the change and the receipt and carefully documents the time and place. He sells the receipt and change to art collectors who then try to track down and purchase Boggs's drawn money from the person who originally received it, creating yet another transaction around the work. He has traveled throughout the world and bought large items, like a motorcycle, with Boggs's Bills. In England and Australia, he's been arrested for counterfeiting, and he is in trouble with the U.S. Secret Service. Every time he gets arrested, the work goes up in value.

I am for art that is political-erotical-mystical, that does something other than sit on its ass in a museum.

CLAES OLDENBURG

The Taxicab Gallery. Thai artist and taxi driver, Navin Rawanchaikul, decided to open a gallery in the back seat of his Bangkok taxicab. Using the cab as the location for a series of conceptual installation pieces by a diverse group of artists, he changes the shows monthly as if he were running a more traditional gallery. Most of the people who enter his taxi are just looking for a ride, but they end up with an unforgettable experience. In response to the increasing interest in the taxi-gallery, Rawanchaikul has printed a detailed schedule of expected daily stops, which he distributes with the disclaimer "times approximate."

Keith Haring. This late New York artist began his career by drawing with chalk on subway walls. Ordinarily, the panels that line the New York subways are filled with ads. One day Keith Haring noticed an empty panel at the Times Square Station and decided to fill it with a drawing. Before long, he was making a drawing in the subway every morning on his way to work. His images became so popular and so many people thanked him for making them that, according to the biography by John Gruen, he "found it difficult to stop. It became a rewarding experience to draw and see the drawings being appreciated. The number of people passing one of these drawings in a week was phenomenal."

The subway drawings had the added effect of launching Haring's very successful art career. By his untimely death in 1990 at the age of thirty-one, Haring's art had moved from the New York subways to the most prestigious galleries and museums in the world. He did not limit his work to the gallery system, however. A champion of art for all people, he also transferred his images to watches, T-shirts, and give-away buttons. Whenever he would arrive in a new city to install a museum show, he would schedule time to create a mural with local children as well. His work has universal appeal and can be found all over the world.

I don't want life to imitate art. I want life to be art.
CARRIE FISHER

Christo and Jeanne-Claude. Renowned for large scale projects that involve wrapping buildings or locations in yards of fabric, Christo and Jeanne-Claude create completely self-financed site-specific environmental art. They and their teams have wrapped a huge government building and a bridge, and they surrounded eleven entire islands in fabric. This is artwork on a grand scale. The creation of each piece involves not just the design, fabrication, and installation of the art, but also years of negotiations with the people who own the property, or use the building, to gain the necessary permissions. They must consider local zoning restrictions and the environmental impact of the project every time they approach a new location.

Then there is the difficulty of financing their work. Obviously, art of this kind is meant to be experienced, rather than owned. You can't exactly carry a wrapped building home and hang it in your living room. The projects are supported in several ways. Christo makes lots of preliminary drawings and collages of a proposed project that they sell themselves rather than through an art dealer. They also sell smaller wrapped sculptures and works they created in association with earlier projects that have increased in value over the years. When a project is complete and dismantled, they recycle the materials, returning them for use elsewhere.

Do you see yourself here? In these examples, the common thread of authenticity and creativity is a combination that can't be beat. No matter how cynical the world becomes, genuine work will always find its audience, but you may have to help it along by stepping outside of your studio. I am reminded of my dear friend Rachel, one of life's originals, who had grown weary of waiting for true love to appear. One day she announced, "I finally figured it out: my white knight can't get his horse into the elevator." She decided to go out and meet him halfway. Not a bad plan.

Success is the child
of audacity.
BENJAMIN DISRAELI

CHAPTER TWO

Creating Your Artist's Packet

In order to approach any of the different kinds of exhibition spaces described in the previous chapter, you will need to assemble an artist's packet. The artist's packet is the basic business tool of the art world; it is the way we make First Contact. A typical artist's packet will include a sheet of slides of the artist's work, a list of past exhibitions called an artist bio, a written statement about the work, a cover letter, reprints of reviews or articles about the art if you have them, exhibition announcements with color images of your art, and a self-addressed stamped envelope (SASE) large enough for the return of your materials, all placed lovingly inside a 9" x 12" or 10" x 13" envelope. It is a good idea to include a stiff piece of cardboard to protect your materials from the exuberance of the post office.

When a gallery receives a packet of slides from an artist, the first thing the staff person notices is whether or not the information is presented in a clear and professional manner. This is a signal that the art work can be expected to be professional as well. If the packet is thrown together in a sloppy or confusing manner, if the slides are of poor quality, if only part of the materials are there, or if the cover letter is insulting, too personal, or too demanding, the gallery will probably send everything back without further consideration.

Put yourself in the gallery director's place. Every week you receive hundreds of slides from hungry young artists who all want *you* to change their lives. You probably enjoy looking at art, that's why you took this job; but you are already working a fifty-hour week and still not getting everything done. You didn't ask to receive these slides. You probably already know lots of artists who are clamoring for your attention, not to mention the artists whose work you have seen elsewhere and would like to pursue. But those unsolicited slides arrive everyday; and when you open the packets, you wonder why you bothered.

According to reports from gallery owners, at least two-thirds of the unsolicited slides they receive do not even approximate the type of art they handle, questions of quality aside. If the artists who sent the slides had invested the time to find out about the gallery, they would have known this. A gallery that features abstract painting will not be interested in ceramic sculpture or handmade jewelry. Sending inappropriate slides not only wastes everyone's time (including yours), but insults the dealer. Galleries, like artists, develop a certain style and voice. They become known for the kind of art they show, which in turn is a reflection of the gallery owners' interests. To expect them to change their style to accommodate your needs is inappropriate and futile.

Another complaint I hear from galleries is that they receive poor quality slides that are too dark, too light, or not clearly labeled. If they have to strain to see the work, they aren't going to bother. It's easier just to slip the slides into their SASE and send them home.

When I ask gallery owners how many artists they eventually take on who make first contact through unsolicited slides, the answer is invariably "very few." This is because only a very small number of the packets galleries receive are both appropriate and clearly presented. Assuming those hurdles are crossed, a gallery owner who likes an artist's work must then decide if the work is of sufficiently high quality to be considered for the gallery. The owner will then want to meet the artist to be certain that he or she is a person the staff feels they can work with, someone who will be willing and able to meet commitments, someone personable enough to invest time and money in.

I will be an artist or nothing!
EUGENE O'NEILL

When you consider all that, it is a miracle any artist ever gets picked up by a gallery at all. And yet they do, all the time. My own experience, and that of my students, is that approximately 10 percent of the unsolicited slides you send out will result in some form of positive response, if they are well presented and appropriately targeted.

The first step in receiving that response is to create an impressive artist's packet. As an artist you should give as much attention to the preparation and presentation of your artist's packet as you do to your art. The packet will stand for you. It should be clear and concise, look professional, and inspire the recipient to want to see more of your art.

Looking Closely at the Artist's Packet

The cover letter. The cover letter is simply a general greeting. Keep it short and direct, avoiding the impulse to embellish it with unnecessary details. When a gallery receives a packet containing slides, it already knows why they were sent. Obviously the sender wants a show, gallery representation, sales, or, preferably, all of the above. The gallery staff members don't have the time or interest in reading a long letter. When they open the packet, they will glance at the cover letter and then move on to looking at the slides, which is what you want them to do anyway.

Here are a couple of sample letters, which I gladly offer for you to copy in whole or in part. The first letter is simple and direct, perfect for sending slides to a gallery when you don't have a recommendation. The second is slightly longer, but even though it contains more information about the work, it is still succinct and businesslike.

February 5, 1998

Mr. B. R. Fingers, Director of Exhibitions
International Museum of Candy Wrappers
900 Fifth Avenue
New York, New York 10007

Dear Mr. Fingers:

I am writing to introduce you to my work. Enclosed is a current bio, a sheet of slides of silver gelatin prints from my "Deep Chocolate" series, a statement about the work, and a review from a recent exhibition.

If you are interested in seeing the work, I would be happy to send additional materials or arrange a studio visit at your convenience.

Thank you for considering my work.

Sincerely,

John Smith

Enc.:   slides
        bio
        statement
        review
        SASE

February 5, 1998

Mr. B. R. Fingers, Director of Exhibitions
International Museum of Candy Wrappers
900 Fifth Avenue
New York, New York 10007

Dear Mr. Fingers:

Jacqueline Onassis suggested that you would be interested in seeing my work. Enclosed are photographic materials representing a selection of recent photographs from my "Deep Chocolate" series. As you will note from my résumé, the work is exhibited regularly in galleries and museums worldwide and has been featured in numerous international publications.

The photographs from the "Deep Chocolate" series are 20" x 24" color-coupler prints available in an edition of ten. If you are interested in the work, I would be happy to send additional slides and materials, or actual prints, for you to look at.

Thank you for considering my work. I look forward to hearing from you.

Sincerely,

John Smith

Enc.:   slides
         bio
         statement
         review
         SASE

Writing your bio. A typical artist's bio is a one- or two-page list of exhibitions and related activities. Headings may include solo exhibitions, group exhibitions, publications, collections, commissions, awards, education, birth place and date (personally, I skip the birth date) and anything else you feel is pertinent. The rule of thumb is to list the most important information first (usually solo exhibitions). Within each category, list the most recent activity first, working your way back in time. Each listing should include the name and location of the show (just the town, you don't need the street address), the title of the show if there was one, and the show dates (month and year). Don't leave out any of this information. When art professionals review your bio, they are looking to see where you have shown your work and when. There should be enough information in the bio for them to follow up on it if they want to.

If your bio looks like this, put away this book; you don't need it, you are doing just fine. If not, file this bio away in your mind under "Something to Shoot For." I include it as an example of what a bio should look like for a professional artist who has an active and successful career.

If your career isn't quite as active as the one above, you will need to modify the standard form to fit your exhibition record. By definition, an artist at the beginning of his or her career will have participated in very few shows. There is no shame in that. As your career progresses, you will be able to fill in more and more of the blanks.

Artists' careers vary. Often an artist will participate in one or two exhibitions, usually affiliated with his or her school, or maybe a juried show or two, but nothing more. Another common pattern is to experience a flurry of interest from galleries, curators, and critics for several years, and then fade from the public eye. Other artists have a show every once in a while, but no steady activity.

Traditionally, the point of the artist's bio is to highlight your exhibition record. Your career should look vigorous and professional. It should indicate that you take a responsible and dedicated attitude toward your art, that you are committed for the long term, and that your art is vital and in demand. If your exhibition record is sketchy or nonexistent, then you will need to examine the other areas of your life that can attest to your commitment. This is where those highly

Your name
address • phone • E-mail • fax

Selected Solo Exhibitions	Venice Biennale Internazionale, Venice, Summer 1997. Documenta, Kassel, Germany, Summer 1997. Whitney Biennial, Whitney Museum of Art, New York, May 1997. Pace Wildenstein Gallery, New York, October 1996. Tate Gallery, London, May 1996. Margo Leavin Gallery, Los Angeles, May 1995.
Selected Group Exhibitions	Museum of Modern Art, "New Acquisitions," New York, January 1998. Centre National d'Art Georges Pompidou, Paris, September 1997. Royal Ontario Museum, "Wild Visions," Toronto, July 1997. Museum of Contemporary Art, Los Angeles, March 1996. Corcoran Gallery of Art, Washington, D.C., January 1996. Institute of Contemporary Art, Boston, November 1995.
Selected Publications and Reviews	*ArtNews* magazine, cover article, February 1997. *Artforum* magazine, article, "Hot Stars on the Rise," April 1996. *New York Times,* "Biennial's Best Kept Secrets," May 5, 1997. *Los Angeles Times,* "Artist of the Year at Margo Leavin," May 2, 1995.
Grants and Awards	MacArthur Fellowship, 1997. Guggenheim Artist Fellowship, 1996. National Endowment for the Arts, Artist Fellowship, 1995. MacDowell Colony Artist in Residence, 1994.
Education	Master of Fine Arts, San Francisco Art Institute, 1990. Bachelor of Arts, University of Houston, 1988.
Born	Dallas, Texas; January 1, 1966.
Represented by	Pace Wildenstein Gallery, 32 East 57th St., New York 10022 Margo Leavin Gallery, 812 N. Robertson, Los Angeles 90069

developed creative skills come in. What is it about you that is unique and interesting? If you can't think of anything, then I suggest the following exercise. I call it "Rediscovering Your Accomplishments."

Pull out a thick stack of paper or a spiral notebook and draw a chart on the top sheet with the following column headings: month and year, residence, job, artwork, classes, travel, hobbies, other. Under the *month and year* heading, write the current month and year, then work your way across the chart, filling in the information for each column. When you have finished, return to the month and year column, writing in last month's date and filling in the columns with the activities that were going on in your life then. Keep working backwards in time, from month to month, year to year. It won't be long before you realize how many wonderful things you have done in your life. You will be amazed at the lifetime of riches you have to draw upon. Now all that remains is for you to put this together in a form that makes people want to see your work.

The one thing to say about art and life is that art is art and life is life, that art is not life and that life is not art.

AD REINHARDT

Month & year	Residence	Job	Artwork	Classes	Travel	Hobbies	Other
March 1998	Aspen, CO	Ski instructor	Ice sculpture of wild birds	Welding at J.C.	——	bird watching	Still reading *War and Peace*
February 1998	Aspen, CO	Ski instructor	Ice sculpture	——	——	Started bird watching	Still reading *War and Peace*
January 1998	Moved to Aspen	Looking	Started ice sculpture	——	——	Obsessing over not having a job	Reading *War and Peace* again
December 1997	Who knows?	Thinking	Sketches on beach	Quit school	Cancun	Water skiing	Reading Batman comics
November 1997	Kansas City	Coffee house	Drawing from models at school	——	——	——	Reading *War and Peace*
October 1997	Kansas City	Coffee house	Drawing from models at school	Chemistry, beginning drawing	——	——	Reading *War and Peace*
September 1997	Kansas City	Coffee house	Taking drawing class	School starts: chemistry major	——	——	Reading *War and Peace*

Tom Mallonee

Born	Presque Isle, Maine, February 19, 1953
Selected Exhibitions	Bucci's, Emeryville, California, February 1992
	Stevenson College, University of California at Santa Cruz, Santa Cruz, California, January 1985
	Lost and Found, Santa Cruz, California, September 1981
Education	Self taught

The Friends of Photography, Ansel Adams Workshop, 1991
Studied under— Morley Baer
                   Ruth Bernard
                   Marilyn Bridges
                   William Christenberry
                   John Sexton

The Friends of Photography, Ansel Adams Workshop, 1982
Studied under— Ansel Adams
                   Roy DeCarava
                   Olivia Parker
                   Arthur Ollman
                   John Sexton
                   Don Worth

The Friends of Photography, Landscape Workshop, 1981
Studied under— Linda Connor
                   Wanda Hammerbeck
                   Ted Orland
                   John Sexton

Publications	Waterscape Series, 16-page catalog for CMS Collaborative, Fountain Consultants, 1988
Affiliations	The Friends of Photography, San Francisco, California. Member, 1979–Present

One of my former students, Tom Mallonee, has generously allowed me to reprint a bio from early in his career, in which he created a format based on his experiences. At the time, Tom had rarely exhibited his photographs, but he was a committed artist and he wanted to emphasize this. Although Tom had no formal degree in art, he had studied with a number of well-known photographers in a workshop format. He decided to emphasize this. The format of this bio is unusual, but it shows a serious commitment to photography.

Another way artists with a sparse exhibition record can improve their bio is to add a category called "Bodies of Work." Here you can list the art you have made at different times in your life, with one or two sentences describing the materials and/or the content. Maybe you spent a summer in Barcelona sketching buildings designed by the architect Antonio Gaudí and then put the drawings away in a drawer. This is a perfect thing to list under "Bodies of Work." Be sure to give the work a title, "The Gaudí Series" for instance, and mention where and when you did the work. Your listing might read: "The Gaudí Series: Twenty pen and ink sketches of the buildings of Antonio Gaudí, Barcelona, Summer 1994."

Jeanne Herbert, another former student, started out as a travel agent. At the time she was composing her first bio, she hadn't exhibited her work anywhere other than in student galleries. She had traveled a lot, mostly to Africa, taking photographs of people in remote villages and tribes, and she would hang her photos informally on the walls of the travel agency where she worked. To create her first bio, she listed her student shows under the category "Selected Exhibitions" and added the shows she had hung at the travel agency, giving them titles and dates. She then created a "Bodies of Work" category and listed each set of photographs she had made on her travels, writing a description next to it. Her next category was "Travel," which showed her wide range of experience, followed by "Education," in which she included receiving her pilot's license along with more conventional educational experiences. The result is a bio that may not follow the standard exhibition format but nevertheless conveys a vital and committed creative life.

JEANNE HERBERT PHOTOGRAPHY

SELECTED EXHIBITIONS

And/Or, John F. Kennedy University, Orinda, California, January 1992

Portraits of C'ote D'Ivoire, Blue World Travel, San Francisco, 1991

Mali, On the Road to Timbuktu, Blue World Travel, San Francisco, 1990

Photographing People, U.C. Berkeley Extension Gallery, San Francisco, May 1989

BODIES OF WORK

Life in a Longhouse, Black & White Photographs, 1991.
    Documentary portraiture of Iban families on the Upper Skrang River, Sarawak, Borneo.

Portraits of Irian Jaya, Black & White and Color Photographs, 1991.
    Documentary portraiture of Asmat and Dani peoples of Irian Jaya.

Barbershops, Color Photographs, 1989–1991.
    From Africa to Oceania, barbers and their places of work.

Chez Bonne Idée, Color Photographs, 1990.
    A study of small businesses in West Africa and the influence of urban art on their shop signs and displays.

Life with the Mbenzele, Black & White and Color Photographs, 1990.
    A study of life in an Mbenzele Pygmy hunting camp in northern Congo.

Portraits of C'ote D'Ivoire, Color Photographs, 1990.
    Portraits of Baoule, Senufo, and Fulani peoples in C'ote D'Ivoire, West Africa.

The Omo, Color Photographs of Southwestern Ethiopia along the Omo River, 1989.

Mali: On the Road to Timbuktu, Color Photographs, 1988.
    A voyage up the Niger River by pirogue and overland to Timbuktu.

TRAVEL

USA, Canada, Mexico, Europe. Africa: Zimbabwe, Zambia, Botswana, Zaire, Congo, Kenya, Tanzania, Ethiopia, Morocco, Egypt, Mali, C'ote D'Ivoire. Asia, Middle East, India, Indonesia, Malaysia, North and South Pacific Islands, Caribbean, South America. Residency: Morocco 1969–1970.

EDUCATION

U.C. Berkeley Extension, Berkeley, California. Associate of Arts, Fine Art Photography, 1991.

Parsons School of Design, New York. Documentary Photography Program in West Africa, 1990.

Honolulu Flying Academy, Honolulu, Hawaii. Private Pilot License, 1972.

Denver University, Denver, Colorado, 1969.

Here is a truly creative bio by well-known video artist Vanalyne Green. It was written as a joking attempt to attain a teaching position. It may not have had any serious intent, but it was the highlight of the College Art Association Conference in 1982, where I came across it.

VANALYNE GREEN
New York, NY

CAREER OBJECTIVE: TENURE IN MY LIFE TIME

Born: Ft. Knox, KY 1948
B.F.A. California Institute of Arts, Valencia, CA 1973
Graduate work, Feminist Studio Workshop, Los Angeles, CA 1974

Tuition scholarships, California State University, Fresno, CA 1968–1972
CAPS Grant in Multi-Media 1982

SUMMARY OF PERFORMANCES 1982:
• Carolee Schneemann's opening. Stood still with no one to talk to for 10 minutes, pretending to be actively engaged with the work.

• Went to political artist's party. Socialized and danced with men as if they looked at women's bodies objectively.

• Went to art opening. When told by woman from New Museum that she had heard of my work, feigned an aura of blasé normality.

• Went to my Group Show opening. Realizing there was absolutely no one there who could do anything for me, continued to smile, act energetic and interested. This, even though snubbed by Brooklyn woman in smart cotton print dress, whose work was priced entirely too high.

PUBLICATIONS:
By the artist: Ten. Five strictly self-promotional, one authentic attempt at critical thinking and four reproductions of work.

About the artist: Twenty. Four reviews to be used over and over again. Four honorable mentions. Some to impress on a résumé and one that must not ever be seen or mentioned.

References available upon request.

Pay attention to the parts of your life that either add to your cachet as an artist or appear to be in conflict with it. Both can be used to your advantage. Perhaps you have a habit of taking photographs of your hotel room whenever you go on vacation. This can be described as a body of work. Or maybe you have a job as a police officer. Don't try to hide these things; this is the stuff that makes you interesting. Suddenly you become mythological: The Cop Who Taught Himself to Paint in Order to Cope with the Stress in His Daily Life. Find a way to get this into the bio. Later, when you have participated in more exhibitions, you can move to a more traditional résumé. At either stage, though, when you add information about yourself that doesn't conform to the basic information usually found in an artist's bio, do it sparingly, and only if it relates to the art itself. Gallery owners don't want to plow through your life history to find out the facts.

Don't even consider lying on your bio. It's not a good idea, and you will probably get caught. Chances are that the day you add a fake solo exhibition at the Metropolitan Museum of Art in New York to your résumé, will be the exact day you hand your bio to the curator's best friend in Toledo, Ohio. The art world may appear vast on the outside, but it is really a tiny little town. You will find that everyone knows everyone else and they do talk.

The artist's statement. Unless you have skills as a writer, you probably would rather not write an artist's statement. You are probably hoping that you can get away with saying that the work stands for itself. In the 1950s an artist was expected to say things like that, but now it just won't fly. Not because it isn't true—a work of art is still, and always will be, a unique experience that defies description. But describing the work is not the point of the artist statement; the purpose of the statement is to make the viewer want to know more about the work.

The artist's statement will be used in a number of ways, including to point the viewer to the concerns you consider to be important in the work, to set a tone for viewing the work, and to help publicists, curators, and critics write about the work. The value of this last cannot be underestimated. A magazine will often decide to write an article simply because the artist's statement arouses their interest. If astounding artwork reaches them that just happens to be accompanied by an interesting statement, particularly if the statement doesn't need much rewriting, it is a combination too good to resist.

The artist's statement should be short. One page is the standard length, but you could go as long as two. For your first draft, plan to write more than you intend to keep so that later you can edit out the parts that feel embarrassing. The easiest course of action is to think of someone specific in your life and pretend that you are speaking to them about your art. Speak as honestly and straightforwardly as you can. No one expects you to be a brilliant writer. You simply need to convey the thoughts and concerns underlying your art that interest you the most, to give the reader insight for looking at the work.

Keep the information as specific as possible. There are certain experiences common to almost every artist that, although they may be powerful and profound for each individual, come across as ordinary to the viewer. For example, almost every artist I know, particularly painters, describe the creative experience as one in which they never know what will happen before they do it, as a series of surprises becoming manifest. You can write this if you want, but then edit it out. It may be true, but it is not specific enough to generate interest in your art.

Be wary of overblown phrases and big ideas, loftily expressed. If your work is about the big issues, and most art is—after all, who wants to devote their life to small ideas?—you need to find a way to speak of these things with feeling, but without pomposity. Be especially careful of using the royal *We*, which speaks for other people. The minute you say, "We all need love," there will be someone who says "What does this guy mean? I don't need love. How dare he say I need love."

Another pitfall in statement writing is to turn the statement into a list of the things you like. "I like to paint flowers." Who cares? We can tell by looking at the painting that you like to paint flowers. (Unless, of course, the painting is of an ambulance. In that case you might be able to get away with it.) What we want to know is why. Did you have a profound childhood experience with a flower, were you impressed by another flower-painting artist, did you read about painting flowers in a book, did a flower save your life? These are things that could grab our interest.

> *Writing is easy: all you do is sit staring at a blank sheet of paper until the drops of blood form on your forehead.*
>
> GENE FOWLER

Some artists work intuitively; others work analytically. If you are one of those who thinks of a project ahead of time, works out the logistics, and then creates the art, you will have a fairly easy time writing your statement. All you have to do is describe the whys and the hows of the project. If you are an artist who goes into the studio and works until you like what you see, however, it may be more difficult to put the experience into words.

I suggest keeping a visual diary with you in the studio as you work. As ideas and phrases come to you, write them down, in part or in whole. Don't worry about your writing style, just get the thoughts down. Your work wants you to understand it; spend time with it, and it will speak to you. Later you can use the ideas as sources for your statement.

One other important use of your statement is to assist you in crystallizing your thoughts about the work. Clarifying your ideas will accelerate your growth as an artist, and you will find yourself grateful when the time comes to discuss your work with curators and critics. You will be able to tell them decisively and intelligently what your work is about.

After you have written your statement, give it to another artist to read; you can read theirs in return. Then try to imagine the other artist's statement applied to your art, and vice versa. If any part of your statement can be applied to his or her work, the statement is not specific enough.

Here are a couple of examples of successful statements. I am including the statement I use for my Flower Series, which, after several rewrites, finally says what I want it to say. There are also statements from two of my former students, Jim Banks and Alexis White, whose writing styles are completely different. Jim Banks photographs the landscape, and his statement is a straightforward description of his work and the feelings leading to it. Alexis was moved to photograph the remains of the many deer she came across in her daily life. She felt a more poetic response was called for in the statement. Each of these writing styles appealed to different editors, and each received positive responses to them. Use these statements only as starting points. Your statement should be a reflection of you, not written to a formula.

There is a right physical size for every idea.

HENRY MOORE

To create the photographs for the Flower Series, I regularly visit the San Francisco Flower Mart to retrieve the flowers merchants throw away. I find it interesting that these flowers, whose worth in our culture is based upon their youth and beauty, are no longer considered to be of value. I collect the flowers from the trash bins and bring them back to the studio to photograph. Working more like a painter or a sculptor than a photographer, I use the flowers as raw material, sometimes painting or reconstructing the flowers themselves. I am particularly interested in the range of responses the flowers exhibit when faced with death. I have found their actions to be as broad and varied as any human response to trauma.

When they are young, all tulips, for example, look essentially the same. But as they grow older, they begin to develop individual personalities. As they start to fade, they may give up and drop over immediately, or actively resist by pushing outward, or try to hang on by wrapping their petals around each other in what appears to be an embrace. It is this last action that most intrigues me. Flowers seem particularly sensitive to each other's presence and appear to create a community when cut and placed in a bowl. They seem to be drawn to some flowers and repelled by others, and will rearrange themselves according to these affinities and resistances. As the series has evolved, it has begun to touch on this pronounced sensitivity to community.

The work has also extended into the area of portraiture. With each batch from the Flower Mart, one or two flowers stand out for their individuality. I try to remain attuned to their changes and to make images that allow them the clearest possible voice. The photographs, then, can be seen in one sense as metaphors for the human condition, and in another, as portraits of another species.

All photographs are shot with a Hassleblad camera and are printed full-frame, the black edge of the negative being an integral part of the image. The intention is for the photograph to stand as a document, as a moment in space and time. The photographs are printed 20" x 24", in editions of 25, on Ektacolor-Plus paper.

JIM BANKS   Statement

My photographs spring from a lifelong fascination with the landscape. This fascination, present even in my earliest memories, has greatly influenced my personal, academic, and professional pursuits, and most significantly, my photography.

The power, mystery, and perfection of the landscape intrigue me, and I seek to unveil and express those qualities in my photographs, rather than document a specific place or time. It is self-evident that the "pristine" or "unspoiled" landscape is threatened and rapidly vanishing. Still, there is inestimable physical, emotional, and spiritual value in the fragments that remain intact. I choose to photograph the inspiring, rather than the dis-heartening, and what remains, rather than what has been lost.

Semi-abstract, my photographs are characterized by graphic compositions, natural elements of design, and a certain amount of ambiguity. They are deceptively simple.

My photographs are large format, selenium-toned, gelatin silver prints. They are available in numbered, limited editions of 200.

ALEXIS M. WHITE

One day I was walking down the trail and I saw a dead deer.

Another day I woke up to the sound of a deer being hit by a car.

Another day I walked out of my house and scared a deer onto the road and it was killed by a car.

Another day there were vultures hovering over a deer that died on my driveway.

Another day I came home and found parts of a deer scattered all over the road, and people were driving over it, and I clearly heard the cracking of bones.

Upon investigation, there are no reasons or explanations, only the fact of life and the fact of death.

Stationery. Each of the components of your packet—your statement, your bio, and the cover letter—will need to be printed on a piece of paper with your name, address, and phone number on it. Thankfully, it is a simple matter to create such stationery yourself on a computer. If you don't want to design it yourself, you can hire a graphic designer to do it for you, but it will cost more. Your stationery should look professional. Make it simple and direct. The point of the stationery is for the recipient to be able to contact you. You want people to think you are a brilliant artist, but be cautious in trying to convey this with your stationery. Avoid adding too many flourishes or using your images on your stationery, because if the stationery draws too much attention, the viewer will judge your work by your stationery, not on the art. Unless you are looking for a job as a designer, this can be death to your art career. On the other hand, if you can find a way to add a subtle touch of individuality, so much the better. It's a delicate balance, and if you're not sure, go with the simplest, most direct approach. The art will shine that much more.

> *Experience is not what happens to you; it is what you do with what happens to you.*
>
> ALDOUS HUXLEY

A self-addressed, stamped envelope. This is what is called an SASE. Whenever you mail slides to anyone include an SASE or they will not be returned. This expensive mistake can also cause unnecessary anxiety as the months go by and you haven't received any responses for your efforts. Galleries receive mounds of unsolicited packets every day, and they can't afford to spend time or money returning them all. So stack the odds in your favor. In every packet, enclose a 9½" x 12½" envelope addressed to yourself, with enough stamps for return postage attached. In the upper left-hand corner, write the return address of the person you sent the slides to originally. I do this because occasionally someone returns my slides without a letter of any kind. I think that is extremely rude, but it happens; if you have several sets of slides out, it becomes difficult to determine who has returned them. Writing the gallery's return address on the SASE saves you this irritation.

Reviews and show announcements from previous exhibitions. These are optional. The point of adding reviews to the packet is to show the person receiving it that your work is already being critically acclaimed. If you don't have any reviews yet, or if the only review you have describes your work in less than respectful terms, don't include it. Everyone gets a bad review from time to time, even the most successful artists, but it is a good idea not to advertise it.

The slide sheet. A sheet of slides should contain up to twenty images of your strongest work. If you have any doubts about the quality of a particular image, leave it out. An art professional who holds up your sheet of slides and likes the first image thinks, "This is great. What else can this artist do?" If the next slide is not so good, is the response, "The second one must have been a mistake"? No. It is, "With one good piece, and then a bad one, this artist must not be able to tell the difference." If you don't have twenty pieces you feel strongly about, just send ten. It is also a good idea not to send more than one sheet of slides, even if you have lots of work. The point of sending slides is to get the gallery's attention, so cull the slides carefully until every one of them is a killer. Anyone who wants to see more will ask.

> *A photograph is a secret about a secret.*
> DIANE ARBUS

If you are an artist who works in several mediums or in more than one style, you have an additional dilemma. Each slide sheet should contain images from only one type of work, and you will have to decide which body of work to send to each recipient. Mixing different kinds of work is one of the first marks of the dilettante and is the kiss of death to your proposal. A gallery wants to know what it is getting when it gives an artist a show. It wants to have a sense of who the artist is and what the work is about, and, being concerned about the bottom line, it wants to have something consistent to market.

When in doubt, send your most recent work; it is probably your strongest anyway. Never send slides of very old work. Gallery owners are interested in what you are doing now, not what you did five years ago. If all you have is old work, I would suggest getting into the studio and working, setting a goal of having enough strong new pieces to fill a slide sheet in six months or a year.

Artist's Packet Check List

____ One or two show announcements with pictures (optional)

____ A short, sweet cover letter

____ One exhibition bio

____ One artist's statement, specifically written to accompany these slides

____ Xerox copies of favorable reviews of your art (optional)

____ One sheet of perfect slides of your art

____ A 9½" x 12½" self-addressed, stamped envelope (SASE) for the return trip

____ A piece of cardboard to protect the packet (placed inside the SASE)

____ A 10" x 13" envelope to put it all in

____ Enough postage to get it there

A Word about the Quality of Your Slides

This is not the place to skimp. I know that spending money on film and processing, and particularly on hiring a professional photographer, can become an expensive proposition, but consider the situation. You have put hours (days, weeks, months, years) into creating your art, and now you are trying to get across the power of the work in a 1" x 1½" piece of film. Focus, lighting, composition, and image quality are all important, and if any one aspect is missing, you've lost your audience.

Good slides should contain the following components:

- Artwork should be photographed on an absolutely neutral background. No trees, buildings, dogs, or posing artists should be visible in the image unless they are an integral part of the art.

- Slides should be properly exposed. White areas should be white, black areas should be black. There should be details visible in the slide wherever there are details in the art.
- Lighting should be even across the surface of the image (especially if it is a flat piece). No area should reflect glare from the light source or have shadows falling across it.

If you can afford it, hire a professional photographer to shoot your slides. If not, keep your lighting setup simple and meter the exposures carefully. Pay attention to the details, and allow time for reshoots.

Hiring a professional photographer. It is not uncommon for photo students to decide to pick up extra cash by shooting artwork. I am sure they think the job is an easy one, and on the surface it looks easy; but photographing art is a specialized practice. It requires a thorough knowledge of the way light reflects on different surfaces, the ability to recognize when small changes in exposure are necessary, and an eye for exact color rendition. Just because a photographer is a professional does not mean he or she knows what to do when it comes to photographing art. I suggest telephoning galleries you respect in your geographic area to ask for names of photographers they recommend. They will probably be able to give you several names. Curators at the local museums will have some leads, too. The nice thing about using museums and galleries as information sources (apart from the opportunity to do some networking) is that they are often on a tight budget and have already sought out the best and cheapest photographers in your area. Regardless of who you choose to work with, be sure it is someone who is willing to work with you until you are satisfied with the results.

When working with a professional photographer, you will find that most of his or her time is spent in setting up the lights and camera and tweaking them for optimum results. Therefore, it is to your advantage to shoot all the different formats of photographs you will need at the same time. I often shoot five 35 mm slides, one black and white negative (for later use in press releases) and several 4" x 5" color transparencies in case a magazine or a book wants to make color

> *Every authentic work of art is a gift offered to the future.*
> ALBERT CAMUS

reproductions. A 4" x 5" transparency provides very high image quality for reproduction and is the standard source used for color printing. To make 4" x 5" transparencies, the photographer will need to have access to a 4" x 5" camera and some experience in using one. Increasingly, with the new technology, magazines are willing to use 35 mm slides for reproduction. My experience in these situations is that the image quality still suffers, however.

Shooting your own slides. If you have a technological bent, you might consider learning to take slides of your artwork yourself. There will be an initial monetary outlay for equipment, but you won't have to pay repeated photographer's fees. And since no one cares about your art more than you do, you will eventually get very good slides. There are several good books dedicated to teaching you how to make slides, but here is a reliable basic plan.

Basic Equipment List:
- *Camera:* You will need a 35 mm single-lens reflex (SLR) camera body with manual exposure capabilities and interchangeable lenses. (Those lightweight travel cameras and fancy cameras with zoom lenses will not work for these purposes.) As a tool, the SLR camera had been perfected by the 1960s; everything that has developed since is just bells and whistles, some of which not only don't help you but often get in your way. Older cameras are fine, but be sure you get a single-lens reflex, not a double-lens or rangefinder camera. When you look through the viewfinder of an SLR camera, you see the image framed exactly as it will be framed in the slide. This is very important: you don't want to cut off the edge of your painting accidentally. If you have a grid focusing screen installed in the viewfinder of the camera, you will be very grateful. A grid focusing screen allows you to see a grid when you look through the viewfinder, which makes squaring up the edges of the artwork much easier.
- *Lens:* Don't buy the normal lens that ordinarily comes with the camera unless you will be photographing sculpture. For flat artwork, you will want a 55 mm or 105 mm macro lens. This has the added advantage of being useful for close-ups as well. The best way

to choose a lens is to go into a camera store and try several of them. Attach one to the camera, then look through the viewfinder at an object roughly the size of your biggest artwork. Focus so that the object exactly fills the frame, and then notice how far away you are standing from it. Will the room in which you plan to work be large enough? If not, change to a lower-millimeter lens, one with a shorter focal length.

Sometimes the salesperson will try to talk you into buying a zoom lens, using the argument that it can do everything. A zoom lens can do everything, but it doesn't do it very well. You will sacrifice sharpness in some areas of the photograph; and while this is okay for travel photographs, it is not okay for your artwork. Do you really want only part of the art to be sharp?

- *Tripod:* Look for a tripod sturdy enough to hold the camera; one that will not be easily knocked over. Try lengthening and shortening the legs a few times. Is it easy to adjust? Put some weight on it. Do the clamps hold?
- *Cable release:* The purpose of the cable release is to eliminate camera shake, particularly when you are using long exposures. Any cable release that fits your camera will do (and they're cheap, too).
- *Tungsten or quartz lights:* Before you buy any lights, I would urge you to go into a full-service photo supply store and have the clerk show you the different levels of lighting available. Tungsten lights are the least expensive. They will do the job, but tungsten light bulbs wear out quickly and change color with use, so always buy two at once, and change them both at the same time. Quartz lights are ideal, but they cost more. They don't overheat, the color balance is consistent, and they are easy to use. Do not let the salesperson talk you into buying a strobe unit. Strobes are fun, but they are difficult to use for photographing art. Because the flash lasts for only a fraction of a second, you can't see the way the light falls on the subject. You will find it difficult to identify problem areas. Some strobes come with modeling lights that are used while setting up a shot, but these are not strong enough to give really detailed information.

If you choose to work with tungsten lights, you will want to get two lights with reflectors. The cheapest approach is to buy a

Go on working, freely and furiously, and you will make progress.

PAUL GAUGUIN

couple of basic 12" clip-on lights at the hardware store. Be sure that they come with a ceramic, rather than a plastic base. The lamps will get hot, and plastic bases can melt and create a fire hazard. You will need a stand for each light (available at photo supply stores) and two 500-watt (3200-degree tungsten) light bulbs.

• *Gray card:* A gray card is exactly that, a piece of cardboard painted evenly with a perfect middle-gray tone. It will assist you in determining the best exposure when you use either the light meter in your camera or a separate reflectance meter. If you are using an incident-light meter, you won't need a gray card.

• *Small level:* I mean a really tiny one. This is for placing on your camera and the artwork to check whether or not they are level. You can buy these at photo supply stores or sometimes at hardware stores. This can save many headaches from trying to figure out why the picture doesn't look straight. A worthwhile investment.

• *Film:* You can use any color slide film that is balanced for tungsten lights. Be careful not to buy daylight film, or your pictures will turn out orange. Films either have the word *color* or the word *chrome* at the end of the name. Ektachrome and Ektacolor are two examples. Avoid the *-color* films. They are for making color prints, not color slides. Choose a chrome film that has a slow film speed (the number behind the name, as in Ektachrome 100). The lower the number, the slower the speed. You want a slow film because it has a higher tonal range, less contrast, and finer grain. A slow film requires a longer exposure time, but this does not matter since you will be using a tripod anyway; unless you make kinetic sculpture, your art won't be moving much.

   Most photographers I know use Ektachrome 64 for shooting artwork. It is fairly slow and can be developed at almost any lab. Stay away from Kodachrome film, because it requires a more delicate development process that usually translates into a longer turnaround time, and sometimes needs be sent to a larger city for processing.

• *Light meter:* If your camera has a light meter in it, and most SLRs do, you won't need to buy a light meter. If your camera doesn't have one, buying a hand-held meter is a must. Hand-held meters come in two types, reflectance and incident. The reflectance meter measures the light as it reflects off the object. The meter inside your camera is a reflectance meter. An incident meter is held near the object to be photographed and measures the light that falls on it. Either will work. I usually use an incident meter, because then I don't need a gray card.

- *Polarizing filters for the lights:* Polarizing filters are not absolutely necessary, but I think they make the difference between mediocre and really good slides. You will need two, since polarizing filters are placed over each light. They cut down on glare, so your colors appear richer and you have fewer hot spots. They work especially well with oil paintings, photographs, and art under glass. Choose a size larger than your reflectors. The 18" size, in a cardboard mount, is a good choice.
- *Stands for the filters:* The filters need to be kept an inch or two away from the lights so that they don't melt. Any cheap photo stand will do the job. You will also need clothespins to clip the filters to the stands.
- *Polarizing filter for the camera:* There is no point in having polarizing filters for the lights if you don't get one for your lens as well. You will adjust the filters in relation to each other.

All great truths begin as blasphemies.
GEORGE BERNARD SHAW

Basic Photographic Procedure:

1. Hang your artwork on the wall. Choose a neutral-colored wall, white or black. I usually hang a big piece of black fabric on the wall behind the art. A black background is less glaring when the finished slides are projected and, in most cases, shows the art to advantage, unless the art is very dark to begin with.

2. Load the camera. Put the camera on the tripod. Attach the cable release.

3. Look through your camera's viewfinder to make sure that your artwork fits inside the frame of the camera viewer. Line up the center of the camera lens to the exact center of the artwork. Then use the level on both pieces to make certain that each one is level to the floor. This will avoid the artwork appearing trapezoidal in the slide.

4. Set up the lights on their stands on either side of the artwork. The center of each light should be at a 45-degree angle to the opposite

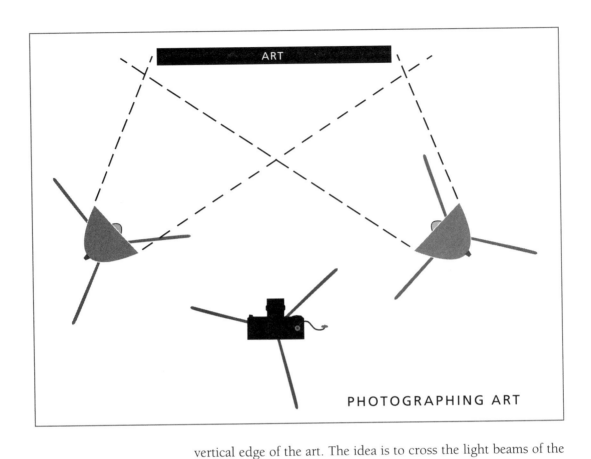

PHOTOGRAPHING ART

vertical edge of the art. The idea is to cross the light beams of the two lights, in order to create an even field of light across the surface of the art. The lights should be placed at least as far away from the artwork as the camera is, but not so far that light strikes the camera itself. This lighting setup is designed for flat surfaces, such as paintings, drawings, or photographs. For sculptural surfaces, start with one light only, placing it slightly to the side of the camera and slightly higher. Notice how the light falls on the object. Adjust the light until it shows the art to its best advantage. Then add other lights as needed. Lighting sculpture can be tricky. It takes patience and attention to detail. There are many good books on the subject.

5. Place the polarizing filters in front of the lights—far enough away not to burn them—and follow the instructions on the filters as to which way is up. The filters will cut down on the amount of light that reaches the artwork, but since the camera is on a tripod you can make up for it by using a slow shutter speed.

6. Put the polarizing filter on your camera. Look through the view-finder and turn the outer ring on the filter; you will see a dramatic difference in the way your artwork looks. Turn the ring until all the hotspots have disappeared and the color intensity is at its best.

7. Next you will need to check the exposure. If you are using the light meter in your camera, you will need to remove the camera temporarily from the tripod to do this; if you are using a hand-held reflectance meter, the camera can stay where it is. Hold up a gray card and your camera (or hand-held light meter) in the center and at all four corners of the artwork, taking a light reading in each spot. Hold the gray card directly in front of the art and parallel to it, and aim the light meter at the card, not at the art. Comparing the readings will tell you if the light is falling evenly over the entire art piece. If all the readings are the same, don't move anything. If not, change the angle or position of the lights—*one at a time* (or you'll go crazy)—until you get a balanced reading. If you have an incident meter, you don't need the gray card. Be careful not to stand between the lights and the art when you are taking meter readings.

8. If you are using the meter inside the camera, the exposure indicated should be correct. I usually set my shutter speed at one second, and then adjust the aperture ring on the lens (the f-stop) as the meter suggests. If you use a hand-held meter, subtract one-and-one-half stops from the exposure reading to compensate for the polarizing filter on the lens.

9. It is always a good idea to bracket exposures to be sure you get a good result. Bracketing exposures is a photographic term meaning to hedge your bets by taking several different exposures of the same thing. It's easy to do. Shoot your first exposure at the proper reading (for instance f-5.6 at one second). Then shoot another at a half-stop overexposed (between f-4 and f-5.6), and a third shot at a half-stop underexposed (between f-5.6 and f-8). Keep the shutter speed the same throughout the procedure. By bracketing, you are bound to get one of your exposures right.

10. Hints to make it easier: Try to cut down on the variables so that, if anything goes wrong, it will be easy to trace. If you always use a one-second shutter speed, you will have maximum latitude in

Content is a glimpse.

WILLEM DE KOONING

choosing your f-stop. Decide on a film, and then stick with it until you know it well. Always use the same processing lab so that you can develop a relationship with the staff. Use the same lighting setup each time. Once you've found the perfect lighting setup, mark the spots on the floor with tape so you'll know exactly where to put the lights next time. If you can, leave the lights set up for a few days so that you can reshoot if you don't like the lab results.

11. Good luck!

Right about now you are probably thinking that it would be easier just to shoot your slides outdoors on a nice day. I don't recommend it. It certainly saves a lot of money and trouble fooling around with lights, but it is almost impossible to control the sun and the sky. You may get lucky and shoot perfect slides the first time, but outside it is impossible to have predictably repeatable results. Even if you are lucky enough to live in a place where the weather never changes, you would still need to be careful to shoot your slides at the same time of day each time. If you don't, they will have a slightly different color tinge since the light at different times of day affects the film differently. If you still want to try shooting outside, use daylight instead of tungsten film, don't forget the polarizing filter on your camera, and watch out for stray shadows.

Making 35 mm slide duplicates. Shoot a minimum of three to five perfect slides of each image. If you are bracketing your exposures, this means that only a third of your slides will be any good, so plan ahead. Make one good set to send off for duplication and another to put into a slide carousel for giving slide lectures; the third set should never ever leave your house. A couple of extra sets of slides are not a bad idea in case of a catastrophe. Keep one set at a friend's house or in a safety deposit box.

Duplicate slides are never as good as the originals, so if you can afford to do so, make more than three sets when you shoot. If you do have to get duplicates made, shop around. Prices and quality can vary dramatically. Duplicates should always be made from originals. Never duplicate other duplicates, or you will lose information in the details and the contrast will become unacceptable. I have named a few companies I have worked with happily in the appendix. I am sure there are many more. Always choose a lab that is willing to work with you until you are happy with the results.

Labeling slides. Label each slide with your name, the title of the piece, the year (with copyright symbol), the work's medium and size, and an arrow showing which way is up. It is a good idea to put your address and phone number on the slide as well, in case it gets separated from the accompanying paperwork. This is a lot of information to crowd into such a small space, but it can be done by printing with very small type onto self-stick labels made especially for slides. Several companies make them, and they can be found in stationery stores. Be sure to get the kind presented on 8½" x 11" backing, so that they will fit your computer's printer.

> *Let your workings*
> *remain a mystery.*
> *Just show people*
> *the results.*
> TAO TE CHING

Unhappily, although the information required on every slide is standard, the placement of it isn't. It seems as though every grant or competition wants the information written in a different order. It is a good idea to leave a few slides unlabeled for these contingencies.

Assembling Your Packet

The packet should be put together with the cover letter on top, followed by your artist's bio, your statement and optional reviews, a sheet of slides, and finally the SASE and cardboard stiffener. If you are including a color announcement, put it on the top of the stack and then affix them all with a paper clip. The idea is to give the recipient a packet that is easy to deal with and shows your work to advantage.

My favorite method for arranging a packet requires that you buy two sizes of envelopes. Use a 9½" x 12½" envelope for your SASE, address and stamp it, and then cut a piece of stiff cardboard to place inside it. Paper-clip your other materials to the outside of the SASE, with the cover letter on top. Put all of this inside of a larger envelope—10" x 13" is a good size. The cardboard protects the materials in transit both ways, and if you place it inside the return envelope yourself it makes it easier for the recipient to return everything intact.

The first time you mail an artist's packet, you will be amazed at how much work it took. Creating and organizing the materials is time-consuming and not nearly as enjoyable as making art. There will probably be several points at which you almost quit; but if you hang in there and complete it, putting together future packets will be a snap.

Now you just have to decide where to send them.

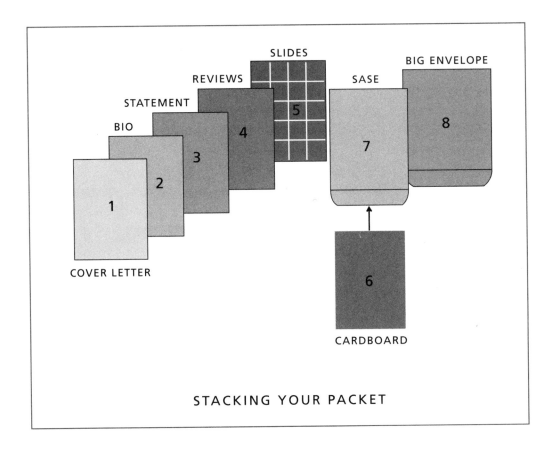

STACKING YOUR PACKET

CHAPTER THREE

*C*hoosing *Y*our *O*wn *L*ife

You have much more control over your life as an artist than many people will have you believe. Traditionally, artists have been encouraged to behave passively concerning their careers, to accept gratefully whatever offers or opportunities happened to come their way and, if there were none, to accept that as well. This tiresome "if you are any good, you will be rewarded" mentality preys on an artist's insecurity about his or her art and offers salvation only through a "fairy gallery owner."

Changing that scenario is not difficult, but before you jump into the art market, let's talk about setting goals. The first and best thing you can do for yourself is to gain some clarity about what you really want. Then you can set about obtaining it.

In planning for the future, your greatest enemy will be the inner voice that tells you it can't be done. As artist and curator Tim Taylor describes it, "We are taught to rehearse the negative." Instead of thinking your goals are impossible, train yourself to ask not "Can I do this?" but "How can I do this?"

Personal insecurities aside, a lot of the ideas we hold about artists come from attitudes embedded in the culture itself. People who are not artists are fond of describing artists as "flaky." They say that we have no head for business and can't function in the real world. They assume we have to suffer for our art, and put the words *starving* and *artist* together so often that even we believe it is our destiny.

In the seven years I have worked with artists, I have found that not only are these concepts wrong, they are monumentally wrong. If artists don't function well in the business world, it is not because they can't but because, for the most part, it holds little interest for them. Artists would rather be making art. When an artist decides to turn his or her attention to business, the results can be amazing. Artists are first and foremost creative people, and creativity applied in any arena transcends whatever apparent limitations there are. Creativity, by definition, changes everything.

As artists, we have been taught to be wary of the business world, and this caution is not without foundation. The business world is not renowned for its concern with the quality of life, questioning the status quo, or any of the deeper issues. The business world is primarily concerned with the bottom line; other issues are considered second, if at all. In order to enter the business world, you will need to learn how it functions. Here are a few guidelines to help you maintain your integrity while learning to negotiate in the realm of business.

I have offended God and mankind because my
work didn't reach the quality it should have.

LEONARDO DA VINCI

Guidelines for Entering the Business World

Make the art first, then find the market for it. It is standard practice in the business world to conduct a market survey prior to launching a new product. This practice may be brilliant if you manufacture baby diapers and need to discover whether your new style works before you invest in producing a million of them. But the efficacy and power of art cannot be measured; certainly not by any survey.

Encountering art is a private experience, specific to the viewer. Since no two viewers are alike, it is impossible to concoct a formula guaranteed to succeed. As an artist, you have to start from yourself—what you know and what you think—and from that make the truest art you can. Then begin searching for your audience, the people who can hear what you are saying. If you make authentic art, art that is meaningful to you, it will speak to someone else.

Don't try to second-guess the market. If you do, one of two things will happen. Either you will guess wrong and end up making art that nobody wants (and you're probably not very interested in either), or you will guess right and spend your life making art you don't want to make while dreaming of the day when you can make your own art again.

The point of being an artist is to make your own art, art that speaks about the things you want to say in the way you want them said. Any business decisions that lead you away from this are the wrong ones.

Assessing your art in terms of the marketplace. Before you enter the marketplace, you will need to take an honest look at your art. Put your emotional attachment aside and look at the work as others see it. One obvious element to examine is quality. Does the work live up to your standards in terms of its concept and the execution of that concept? Most artists are never completely satisfied with the quality of their work. In their eyes, there is always something that can be improved. Taking that into consideration, does your art live up to the ideals you have set for it? Is it at least as well-made as other works of the same genre that are selling in galleries? If it is almost there but not quite, get

> *Better to write for yourself and have no public, than to write for the public and have no self.*
> CYRIL CONNOLLY

back to work. Don't let your art leave the studio until you are 97 percent happy with it (the other 3 percent can be attributed to intrinsic artist dissatisfaction).

Christine Normile, codirector of the Sherry Frumkin Gallery in Los Angeles, says that an artist presenting work "has to be 200 percent open to criticism, because that is absolutely going to happen." If your art can't withstand your own examination, you will find it difficult to deal with the scrutiny of others.

Let's assume you are happy with the quality of your work. The next thing you need to consider is where your art fits in the marketplace. Who is your audience?

In the first chapter, I suggested that you think of art history as a centuries-long conversation. Each generation of artists comes along, listens to what has been said before, and then adds something new. You might also think of it as an extended cocktail party; and just like any cocktail party, if you jump in and say something that somebody else has already said, you will probably be ignored.

Who attends this party? Museum curators, art historians, critics, high-profile gallery owners. These people want to see art that is cutting edge, art that surprises them, art that takes the culture's knowledge of itself in a new direction, or art that moves an old direction in a new way.

If this is the kind of art you make, if these are your goals too, then this is the market you should aim for. If your work is truly saying something new, then don't be shy about sending your work to the well-known galleries, the world-class museums, and the most demanding critics. If your art isn't saying something new, don't waste your time trying to get these people to pay attention to you.

Most art isn't about breaking new ground. Many artists create for the love of the materials; the thrill of putting paint to canvas; the joy of capturing a moment, person, or place in every detail; or the challenge of pushing oneself to master techniques used by the great artists of antiquity. Museum curators and art historians may call this derivative art because it is covering ground already attended to by earlier artists, but for the artists making it, it is as fresh and true as any art can be.

Maybe you are making beautiful paintings in the style of Monet, or

A life spent making mistakes is not only more honorable, but more useful than a life spent doing nothing.

GEORGE BERNARD SHAW

exploring the beauty of nature, the human figure, personal growth, or spirituality in a manner that is not new to the art world but is authentic to you. Maybe your focus is on painstaking craftsmanship. These are all worthy of your attention, and there are markets for all of them. There are thousands of galleries, as well as local museums and non-profit spaces, that specialize in each of these genres. Much of this kind of art can be sold through art consultants as well.

Making strategic choices. The quickest way to reach success is to narrow your list of goals, just for the short term. I know you want *everything*, but which part of everything do you want first? Do you want to get your work seen or do you want it to be sold? Do you want gallery representation? Do you want to show in nonprofit spaces? University galleries? Is gaining notoriety important? The choices you make in these areas will determine where and how you approach your market.

How I Learned to Set Goals

Several years ago I took a class at UCLA called the Psychology of Success. I had finished art school and was supposed to be building a body of artwork, but I couldn't seem to make myself work. I would start a piece and not finish it. I would buy a new set of art materials and use them once. I wanted to be an artist more than anything; I agonized every day over my inability to get anything done. Then I noticed the Psychology of Success class in the UCLA Extension catalog.

> *I don't know the key to success, but the key to failure is trying to please everybody.*
>
> BILL COSBY

The class was in one of those big circular auditoriums with the professor standing in a glow of light in the front. There must have been five hundred people there, or so it seemed at the time. On the first day, the teacher passed around a box of 3" x 5" cards and asked all of us to write our goals on a card. When my turn came I thought, okay, no more thinking small for me, I'm going to think big. So I wrote: "I want to be really famous."

We returned the cards, and the teacher shuffled through them, plucked one out, and held it high. She announced with authority, "This person is doomed to failure."

You probably know what's coming, but I didn't. I thought, "Oh, that poor person!" Then she read *my* card aloud to the whole class. I could have kept my anonymity, but I was so appalled that I whined loud enough for everyone to hear, "Some people are famous. Why can't it be me?" The teacher turned to the class and asked them if they knew why my goal could never be achieved. Fortunately, for my ego, only one person knew the answer.

The answer is: Because you can't figure out the first step! It's fine to want to be famous, but famous for what? Baseball? Piano playing? Inventing a new adhesive? I had neglected to state my area of interest. Also, what do I mean by *really* famous? How much is really? How would I measure it? A solo show in a museum? Which museum? My own TV show? A breakfast cereal named after me? Dinner in my honor at the White House?

So when you sit down to set your goals, make them specific. The more precise they are, the more obvious the first step will be to you. If you want to be a respected painter, the first step obviously is to paint. Think about what you mean by respected. Whose respect do you want? What do you want to have achieved to merit this respect? The more specific the questions, the more obvious the answers, and the easier it will be to achieve goals.

I learned many amazing things in that class. The teacher described an experiment in which they placed a rat at one end of a chute and its food at the other, and then measured how fast the rat ran to the food. The scientists discovered that no matter how long the chute was, no matter how far the rat had already run, it always found an extra burst of energy the minute the goal was in sight. The teacher described this as an adrenaline rush.

Have you ever noticed that when you have twenty phone calls to make you can put them off indefinitely? And yet, once you make the first call, the others seem to follow with ease. This is the best part of an adrenaline rush, the overflow of energy that automatically propels you on to the next task. You can use this phenomenon to your advantage.

It is good and right to set big goals for your life's plan; all successful people have them. But exceptionally successful people make sure their days are filled with lots of little goals as well. Every time they complete a goal, they experience the extra boost of energy that comes with achievement. Every time you achieve another goal, you feel good

I find it rather easy to portray a businessman. Being bland, rather cruel, and incompetent comes naturally to me.

JOHN CLEESE

about how much you have accomplished; and that is so much more enjoyable than feeling bad about how much you haven't done.

Say you want to become really buff; you want your whole body to become a solid mass of muscle. Obviously, the first step is to set up an exercise program. Let's assume it's a big job—you're thirty pounds overweight and not exactly in shape. You decide to go to the gym and work out two hours a day, seven days a week for the next three years. This is just setting yourself up for failure. Who can go to the gym every day for three years? You are bound to let yourself down. It is not that your goal is too big, but the steps are. The best way to set up a daily goal is to ask yourself what you can realistically do, given your lifestyle and circumstances, and then cut that number in half. You will get a lot more out of yourself, and feel a lot better doing it.

So you have been meaning to go for a run before work in the morning, but you can't seem to get started. Change the goal. Instead of setting a goal of running every morning, decide you just have to get into your running clothes. Once you put on the outfit, you will often find that you might as well take a short run. But on days when you don't, on days when you just get into the outfit and take it right off again, congratulate yourself. You achieved your goal; running was a bonus.

You can use this same kind of thinking for your art career. Maybe you want to paint a masterpiece to rival Picasso's *Guernica*. There's a nice big goal! First of all, how do you measure a masterpiece? You can't. If you can't be sure you are creating a masterpiece, what can you be sure of? You can be fairly certain that you are making a painting. And you can be fairly certain that making a painting is how Picasso started.

If you are a painter, set a goal to be in the studio painting a certain number of hours per week. Watch yourself the first week to see if you are meeting your goal. If you are not, don't scold yourself for being a shiftless sloth with the backbone of boiled pasta. Change the goal to one you *can* meet. Decide that all you have to do is be in the studio; you don't have to actually paint anything if you don't feel like it. All you have to do is be there. Eventually you will pick up a brush, out of boredom if nothing else. Do whatever it takes to reach the point where you start to develop a regular pattern, no matter how elementary. Before long, the thrill of the work will carry the momentum for you.

Anyone who says businessmen deal in facts, not fiction, has never read old five-year projections.

MALCOLM FORBES

In my classes, the students set their own goals for studio time. Some work for as little as one hour a week, others as many as forty-five hours a week (those are the ones with the trust funds). It doesn't matter what goal is set, as long as it is reachable for the artist who set it. After two weeks, we reassess the goals. If an artist is easily reaching or surpassing his or her goal, we leave it as it is. If the artist really had to stretch to make it, or simply couldn't, we cut it in half. There is no shame in setting a small goal. Each of us has different responsibilities, different demands on our time. Instead of growing angry over your circumstances, or making yourself *wrong*, accept the cards you were dealt and start from there. Even with just an hour a week, if it is honored every week, an amazing amount can be accomplished.

One of my students, a young lawyer, hated her fifty-hour-a-week job. All she wanted to do was paint. Her job was so demanding that she only had one day off a week, and that was usually consumed by necessary chores like laundry and grocery shopping. She decided to carve two hours out of that day for painting. Some weeks she was able to do more, but she always stuck to her two-hour minimum. After a couple of years, she was able to build a body of work and to begin exhibiting and selling her paintings. Then she reduced her hours at the office, and recently she quit her job altogether. I've never seen anyone happier. It all started with making a commitment to her art that she could actually keep, and then building from there.

To help you define your goals as an artist, I have included a one-page questionnaire, a self-contract, for your use. Don't agonize over filling it out; you probably already know most of the answers. The idea is to clarify your goals, not to create an excuse to avoid them. If you don't know what your five-year goal is, write whatever comes to mind. You can always change it later on.

Now that you know what you want, you are ready to devise a strategy.

Putting off an easy thing makes it hard, and putting off a hard thing makes it impossible.

GEORGE LORIMER

Name _____ Date:_____

The purpose of this contract is to help you analyze and clarify your objectives and to set goals. Try to be as specific as possible about what you want.

What is success to you? Possibilities include, but are not limited to: creating a new body of work, completing a body of work already begun, finding a new direction as an artist, having a solo show, having a university exhibition (or nonprofit space, or gallery, or museum show), selling work, getting published in a magazine or book, getting a grant, funding a special project, working with art consultants, finding a dealer, getting a gallery in Europe, having five shows a year, ten shows a year, a show at the Whitney, your own TV show, etc.

Not all of these things are possible at the beginning of an artist's career. It depends upon a number of factors: how resolved your art is, how much and where you have shown already, how much time and money you have to devote to your art, and how lucky you get. But don't let that deter you. Set the goals you really want. Setting a goal is always the first step toward getting there.

1. *What is my lifetime goal as an artist?* List everything you can think of here. Be as specific as possible.

2. *What is my five year goal as an artist?* Where would you like to be in five years? Cut down on your lifetime-goal list a bit. Choose the goals you most want to achieve. State them as specifically if possible.

3. *What do I plan to accomplish during the next six months?* Here is where you plan where your energies will go during the immediate time period.

4. *How much time do I plan to devote to my goals each week?* Don't skip this question. It is crucial. Decide how much time you can give to your career as an artist. Decide when you can work on it and where.

*P*lanning a *S*trategy

CALVIN AND HOBBES Bill Watterson

Once you have a body of work completed (or a body of work that is nearing completion) and you have made a few decisions regarding your career objectives, you can start developing a strategy. A good business strategy is one that provides a clear route for reaching your goals, involves the smallest amount of anxiety on your part, and includes lots of small achievements along the way so it feels more like fun than work.

The first thing to remember is that all roads lead somewhere; the second is that you can never be certain just where they are going to lead. An artist may have a show in an uptown gallery and another in a small café. Logic would dictate that the gallery show would be the one to launch the career, and usually that is the case, but not always. I've seen many careers suddenly skyrocket because an influential curator or collector found the art in some offbeat place, and I've heard just as many stories of art languishing unsold in gallery back rooms. For myself, even though my art has been represented by reputable galleries in cities such as New York, London, Paris, Los Angeles, and Houston, it was a café show in Emeryville, California, that led to my work being included in two important collections. The owner of the café was a friend, but when she invited me to show my work, I replied that I was much too important an artist for such a lowly venue. She told me to get off it and bring her some art. So I did. As it happened, two curators had dinner at the café that evening, one from a major museum and the other in charge of a world-class private collection. They saw the work, liked it, and asked me to send them slides.

No formula is guaranteed to work. Since there is no way to do something exactly right, it follows that there is also no way to do it exactly wrong. The only thing you can do wrong is to do nothing at all. Any strategy you choose will take you in the direction of your goal. Some directions will move faster, and some will travel only so far and then stop, requiring that you devise an alternate plan; others will start to lead one way and suddenly veer toward another route. Just stay on that pony, keeping the goal in mind, and you will get there.

I heard a wonderful quote on the radio. I wish I knew who said it. I was driving along listening to music when I changed the channel and heard a man say, "One day I discovered that although two wrongs may not make a right, three left turns do." Since I was driving, I decided to test it out. It works; three left turns *do* make a right. So keep the goal in mind, and you will eventually reach it.

Once I make up my mind, I'm full of indecision.
OSCAR LEVANT

Some Common Strategies

Let's consider some possible strategies and where you can reasonably expect them to lead.

Entering juried shows. Most artists begin their careers by entering competitions. The terms *competition* and *juried show* are used interchangeably in the art world. The artist submits slides of his or her art

Juror Tells All!

By Cay Lang

I have sat as a juror for a number of competitions, and here is what it is like from the other side. Usually the job involves spending one, usually two, and sometimes more days sitting on folding chairs in the dark looking at slides with the other jurors. A juror is usually paid a small stipend as a token for the time invested, but it is nowhere near an hourly wage. The reason a juror agrees to spend several days looking at slides is not for the money, but because he or she feels a commitment to helping the larger art community. The jurors arrive on the agreed upon date, are introduced to each other, make small talk for a few minutes, maybe eat a donut or a bagel, and then everyone gets down to work.

Prior to jurying day, each prospective artist has been assigned a number to prevent the jurors from being influenced by the artist's name, and his or her slides have been placed in carousels, ready for projection. If, as in the case with the now-crippled NEA, the artist was instructed to submit ten slides, there will be five projectors sitting in a row, so that the work of each artist can be viewed as a body, in two sets of five.

The jurors are instructed to vote on the work as it comes up, by number. As they look at the slides, they write their vote on the form in front of them. Often the slides are projected for only a few seconds, and unless one of the jurors asks a question, this brief look is all the jurors get. Even at that speed, it can take hours to view all the slides.

Slides are the great equalizer. If the slides are improperly exposed, even by a tiny fraction, the work will look gray or white or black on the screen, instead of the colors that were originally intended. If the juror has been looking at slides for even just a couple of hours, his or her eyes will not be able to adjust quickly to allow for this deviant information. Since they are viewing so much art, most jurors will tend to dismiss bad slides, turning their attention to the next artist instead.

The problem with slides is that all art is altered by the slide film itself. Art with strong graphic components and rich colors will look even more striking. Images with subtle colors, delicate shadings, or light pencil lines will tend to look muddy or washed-out. Film exaggerates some things and misses others entirely. If the work is conceptual or narrative in nature, or kinetic, or is composed of a lot of text, you will have difficulty trying to capture these details in a tiny slide. Always project your slides yourself before sending them to a competition. Any problems will become apparent immediately.

All the slides are projected to the same size on the wall. This means that a painting thirty feet long will appear the same size as one that measures six inches. If scale is important in your work, you need to make special note of that in the accompanying paperwork. Do not stand next to the artwork; the jurors will look at you instead of the art.

The jurors work like this for three or four hours, looking and voting, looking and voting. They take a short lunch break, and then return to view slides for another four hours. By the end of the day, the jurors have seen more art than they can possibly absorb. To be fair to the organizers of juried shows, most try to be fair to each contestant and show the artists' work in a good light, and they try to create a pleasant experience for the jurors. But the truth is, with hundreds, sometimes thousands of artists applying, there really is no other way to do it.

along with an entrance fee, and a jury decides whether or not to accept the work into the show. If the artist is accepted, he or she will be asked to frame and ship the work. The work will then be exhibited in a group show. Such exhibitions are good for adding entries to your bio, and, who knows, you might win some prize money. You can find juried shows listed in the back of magazines like *Artweek, New Art Examiner,* and *ArtCalendar,* among others.

Entering competitions can become costly. The entrance fees add up, as do framing and shipping costs. And although it is always advantageous to add another exhibition to your bio, juried shows hold the lowest rung on the ladder of art-world status. Enter a few for the experience, if you like, but start planning some more active tactics for launching your career.

You should know how juried shows work. The sponsors collect money from lots of artists, reject most of them, and select a few for inclusion in the exhibition. A small part of the money collected sometimes goes to prizes for a small number of artists, and the bulk of the money goes to the organizers of the show. Sometimes the money goes to support a worthwhile organization, such as a nonprofit art space; but sometimes a juried show is just a scam. It is often difficult to tell the two apart. Just because a juried show is advertised nationally is no guarantee that it is legitimate; sometimes the splashiest shows are the dishonest ones. *ArtCalendar* magazine often prints articles exposing the most obvious scams, but they can't catch them all.

If you decide to enter a juried show, choose carefully. Examine the list of jurors. Are they people you know and respect? What are their credentials? If they are curators, critics, or gallery owners, then entering the competition might be a way to bring your work to their attention. Be aware that they will be looking at hundreds of artworks in a very brief time, so they won't be able to focus on any one artist.

Notice the location of the exhibition. Will the art be exhibited in a museum or someone's garage? One of the reasons for entering a juried show is to strengthen your résumé. If the exhibition will be held at a location that won't enrich your bio, then it is probably not worth it.

You should also consider the cost of a juried show. Look at similar juried-show listings. Is the entry fee about the same? At the time of this writing, five dollars a slide is about standard. If the sponsor is asking very much more, it could be a questionable investment.

Finding a commercial gallery to represent you. The traditional path for entering the art world is to find a gallery to handle your work. This can have many advantages, as we discussed in earlier chapters; but today's artist needs to be much more savvy than his or her predecessors, both in the strategy for finding the gallery, and in working with it once a relationship is established. For one thing, there are many more artists than there are galleries to handle them. Also, the economic climate is more difficult than it was ten years ago, forcing the galleries to pay close attention to their bottom line.

The standard strategy for finding a gallery is to blanket the art world with sheets of your slides, hoping by the sheer numbers to get a bite or two. I asked gallery owners across the country what it is like to be on the receiving end of these truckloads of slides. Their experiences were almost identical in every case. Here's what they told me:

- Most of the slides they receive are from artists who haven't a clue what the gallery is about or from artists who have never seen the space, never heard of the artists they represent, and never attended an opening.
- Much of the material they receive is put together without care or concern: the slides are poor, the labels are nonexistent or incomplete, or the written material is full of extraneous information, such as how much the artist loved a third grade teacher.
- Artists send materials without bothering to inquire about the gallery's facilities for handling them. As one New York dealer pointed out, galleries are ill-prepared to take care of material that does not belong to them, so every gallery has their own solution for looking at slides. Artists will send CD-ROMs and videos to galleries that have no facilities for looking at them, or drop off large portfolios at galleries where space is at a premium, when, with a simple phone call, they could have devised a more effective plan.
- In spite of the difficulties, most galleries consider viewing artist's slides an integral part of their job. When art floats across a dealer's

There is only one success...to be able to spend your life in your own way, and not to give others absurd maddening claims upon it.
CHRISTOPHER MORLEY

desk that is both appropriate for the gallery and presented professionally, it stands out from the multitudes.

It is no wonder that galleries rarely take on artists from unsolicited slides, but I know that the system works when properly applied because it worked for me with several very good galleries early in my career, and because I see it work every year for many of my students. The secret is to choose the recipients of your slides carefully, create beautifully presented promotional materials, and behave in a thoroughly professional manner.

I asked the gallery owners where they get most of their artists, if not from slides. Those answers, too, were instructive. At the top of the list were individuals recommended by artists they represent. As one dealer put it, "If Roy Lichtenstein calls me and says 'there's this young artist and I think she's talented,' don't you think I'm going to pay attention? Of course I am." Gallery owners trust their artists because the artists know what the gallery's program is and the gallery owner knows that the artist wouldn't recommend anyone they would be embarrassed showing with. Gallery owners also listen to recommendations from respected curators and art dealers in other cities with whom they have worked in the past.

Art dealers are always looking; they like to keep an eye on the hottest art-world developments. When they travel, they look at art. In their own town, they look at art. They make a point of seeing shows at all the local noncommercial art spaces. They keep an eye on the artists handled by their competitors as well, although most are quick to say they would never steal an artist from another dealer. They read the art magazines and the newspapers for reviews about artists. And most of them have a long list of dream artists they would like to handle.

Established galleries already have a stable of artists they have invested time and money in, but each gallery can only handle so many artists. The older the gallery is, the less likely they will be interested in unknown artists. As a gallery grows, its focus becomes more definite, and the energies of the staff are directed toward artists whose careers they are already committed to. Younger galleries are more open to taking on emerging artists.

I asked the gallery owners for the best strategies for finding gallery

How much time we lose in seeking our daily bread!

PAUL GAUGUIN

representation, and they listed the following. Suggestion number one was universally to make astounding art. After that, they said:

- Create your own energy. Taking your destiny into your own hands is the key. Really interesting art scenes are created when a group of like-minded artists get together and hang their art wherever they can.
- Become involved in your local (or regional) art community. Go to galleries, attend openings, and meet the people there. If there is a particular gallery you feel would be right for your work, make a point of demonstrating your interest by going to the openings and taking the opportunity to get to know the artists and the dealer.
- Be professional. Make sure everything about your presentation is absolutely top-notch, research a gallery before you approach it, and treat the gallery staff with consideration and respect.

Starting locally. Traditional art-world thinking demands that you start locally. The idea is to build your career by gaining acceptance in your hometown first; as your acceptance grows, so will your career, in an ever-increasing spiral. While this has been the default strategy of artists for centuries, beware, because sometimes you can dead-end at the local level. There are a number of reasons for this. Sometimes an artist's work speaks to a wider or different audience than the one found in his or her immediate geographical location, but the artist who only tries showing the work in that one spot may never become aware of that fact. Also, being a homegrown artist may have a detrimental, rather than a positive, effect. Local artists are a dime a dozen, no matter where you live. It is notoriously difficult to convince people who have grown up with you that you may be a genius. No one ever believes that they could actually know one.

On the other hand, you can usually find a gallery in every town that specializes in local artists. These galleries have a mission to support local art; they like to be able to work directly with artists on a daily basis, and they believe in the talent that surrounds them. For the emotional support, and the chance at some sales, a local gallery of this kind could be a good first move. If the gallery also has connections with galleries in other cities, it could be a great first move.

I have the feeling that I've seen everything, but failed to notice the elephants.
ANTON CHEKHOV

Showing in cafés and other non–art-world spaces. This can be a won-derful way to get started. When you show in a neighborhood café, your friends and acquaintances often get to see your work for the first time. Viewing the art on the walls can be their motivation for buying the work, so you may make your first sales. Cafés are less forbidding than galleries and can create dialogue and interaction around the work. A show in a café usually won't directly advance your career, but you never know who will see it. It could be one of those left turns that leads to the right. Be prepared to do all the work yourself, from hang-ing the show, to publicity, to putting on a reception, to dealing with sales and insurance. Many café-style venues do not take a percentage of sales, so if you sell anything the money is all yours. Of course, they don't have any salespeople pushing the work either, so you deserve it.

Café shows can be a good experience and worth doing a few times, but just like juried shows, they can be a dead-end for your career. Do them for the fun of it and to connect with your neighborhood, but make some steps in other directions as well.

Moving to New York. What about moving directly to New York? When I was a student in art school, I was repeatedly told that if I were truly serious about becoming an artist, I would move to New York. I was willing to tear myself away from California, but my life conspired against it and I became an artist without the benefit of the Manhattan experience. Because the cost of living in California was low, I was able to travel; and before long, I began exhibiting my art all over the world, including New York.

Some of my school friends did move to New York. A few of them were able to launch successful art careers, but most are still waiting. I actually got my first show in an uptown gallery before any of my New York friends did. In Manhattan, every other cabby, waiter, bartender, or salesperson is an aspiring artist, actor, playwright, or novelist, so the competition is very steep. In addition, the cost of living is high. If you move to New York, you will be spending more for food, housing, and even art supplies. Many aspiring artists move to New York with-out a job, a place to live, or money in the bank. This generally results in their finding one of the low-paying jobs above, working long hours,

I think perhaps there would be more anxiety in my work if I lived in New York.

ED RUSCHA

and squeezing in time to make art. If you are young, healthy, determined, energetic, and adventurous, or if you happen to have a nice fat trust fund, go for it.

The truth is, New York is still the hub of the art world. In New York, art movements come and go so fast that the rest of the world rarely even hears about them. There is a cornucopia of art events to choose from; lots of chances to talk and think about art and many opportunities to network. The artistic stimulation alone can be worth making the choice. The stakes are high in New York, but if you are one of the few who make it big, you can make it very big, indeed. Most of the art magazines are located there, as well as several world-class newspapers, so the chance for media attention is much higher than anywhere else. New York also houses more museums, more galleries, and more art collectors. The rich and famous are everywhere; you could become one of them. Just remember, the very poor are everywhere, too.

All the really good ideas I ever had came to me while I was milking a cow.
GRANT WOOD

Jim Pomeroy used to tell a story about John Baldessari at the early part of his career. I don't know if the story is true, but I love it anyway. Pomeroy said that even though John Baldessari lived in Los Angeles, he would fly to New York every couple of months for the art gallery openings. People in New York thought he lived there. They would see him and say, "Hey John, I haven't seen you around for awhile. Where have you been?" And he would answer, "Just working in my studio." He neglected to tell them that the studio was in L.A.

Targeting a large American city. One effective plan is to target a city with an active arts community, devising your strategy from home. Choose any city with a large number of galleries, museums, and non-profit spaces. Some of the more obvious choices are Chicago, Los Angeles, Santa Fe, Seattle, and of course, New York.

The secret to success with this plan, as with all the others, is do your research. Doing your research means finding out as much information as you can about each of the galleries you are considering. You will want to know what kind of art they show, which artists they handle, if they are open to taking on unknown and emerging artists, what the space looks and feels like, and what kind of reputation the gallery has in the community. A good starting point for this information is the August issue of *Art in America* magazine, its Annual Guide to Museums, Galleries and Artists. You can purchase it as part of a subscription to *Art in America*, or pick it up separately at a newsstand. Inside you will find detailed listings of galleries throughout the country, including the name and address, phone, and contact person, the kind of work the gallery shows, which artists it represents, and the exhibitions it has mounted over the past year. There is also quite a long list of art consultants in the back of the magazine.

There are lots of other art magazines, too, each of them carrying articles about art, artists, and the art world. Make a trip to your local library, or an international magazine stand, to find them. Another resource, found in the reference section of the library, is a book called the *Art Index*, which alphabetically lists articles written about every art topic in American magazines. A good guide to New York galleries can be found in the book *New York Contemporary Art Galleries* by Renee Phillips.

Once you have completed the preliminary research, the best strategy is to make a reconnaissance mission to the city you have chosen. Visit the galleries, view the exhibitions, chat up the staff members. When you walk into a gallery, you will be able to make assessments concerning the feel of the space, the attitude of the personnel, and the quality of the installation that would be impossible from a distance. If the gallery passes your inspection, keep it on your list. If not, you have saved yourself a lot of unfruitful work. This trip is also a great way to discover galleries you didn't already know about. Since not all galleries are listed in *Art in America*, you may arrive at one gallery on your list and discover one next door you like better.

When you have arrived at a list of appropriate exhibition spaces, plan a second trip to your chosen city. This time you are going on an earnest search for suitable venues for your art. Write ahead to each prospective exhibition space. Your artist packet should contain a full set of information about you (slides, bio, statement, reviews) and a cover letter asking for an appointment. The idea is to stimulate the gallery's appetite with slides of your incredible art, then set up a time frame for them to view the work itself. If they want to see it, they need to make a decision to take action. Mail the slides about three weeks prior to your trip. Galleries who are not interested in your work will have time to return the slides, and the ones who are interested have a chance to call you to schedule an appointment before you leave home. Galleries have a predictable cycle they go through each month; first they frantically hang the show, then they spend several weeks selling art and tending to other details, then they take the show down and frantically hang the next. If possible, plan your trip to coincide with their slow times and expect to be there a minimum of a week; two weeks is better.

A sample cover letter for a trip to another city follows. Use it as a guide for making first contact.

As soon as you arrive, telephone the galleries. Making these phone calls early in your trip will save you from experiencing the agony of being rejected in person. Not everyone will want to see you, but some will. If they are not interested in your work, ask them if they know of anyone in town who might be. Ask for the correct spelling of the name and the phone number. Then call that person, too.

Upon arriving at the galleries, pick up a copy of the local Art Guide. It will list current exhibitions and galleries that weren't listed in *Art in America* you might want to contact. If you have targeted places appropriate for your work, you should come home with at least one commitment and several maybes. You will get lots of rejections, too. File them under "So what?" You are on your way.

Targeting a foreign city. Different parts of the world have different practices regarding business and art, but don't let that slow you down. When approaching a foreign city, do as much research and preparation as you can and send out your packet of slides; then just trot your pony on over there. You will make some mistakes, but you will also discover that you are doing a lot of things right. An attitude of adventure, forthrightness, and consideration can carry you a long way.

Researching art galleries in other parts of the world can be more convoluted than finding galleries in the United States. There is no European counterpart to the August issue of *Art in America*, but there are many international art magazines and some of them are available

Every work of art is the child of its time; each period produces an art of its own, which cannot be repeated.

WASSILY KANDINSKY

Date

Name
Address

Dear *(Important Person You Are Trying to Contact)*:

Please consider my art for your gallery. I am an artist from *(name your town, state, or country)* making a trip to Seattle in March. I would love to show you my work at that time.

I will be in Seattle from March 5 to 15. My hotel is the Lucky Lucy Travel Inn, at *(give phone number)*. I will call you when I reach town to arrange an appointment. I look forward to meeting you. Thank you in advance for your consideration.

Sincerely,

(Important Person Sending This Letter)

in the United States. A good source for these is an international news-stand, as well as the art library at your local university. When you peruse these magazines, pay as much attention to the ads as the articles. You may even find a gallery guide in the back of the periodical. Think of everything in the magazine as a clue. You can also try contacting the country's consulate for gallery and museum listings. If you are a photographer, you are in luck. Nazraeli Press published three very important books in 1995 and 1996: *USA Photography Guide, European Photography Guide,* and *Japanese Photography Guide.* These books are indispensable for photographers. Unfortunately there is no similar publication for other kinds of artists.

No guts, no glory.

BETTE DAVIS

Once you have compiled your list of galleries, proceed just as you would for any American town. Send the gallery director or curator a slide packet with a cover letter providing your trip dates and a contact phone number. If you are on a tight budget, you might consider sending a smaller packet with fewer slides, since international postal rates are more expensive than domestic rates.

It is a good idea to have your cover letter and artist statement translated into the language of the country you are visiting, particularly if you don't speak that language. That way, if you have to resort to sign language to communicate, you can at least hand them a document they can understand. Translators can be found in the language departments of any university, usually for very little money. You can also find them in the yellow pages.

The first time I took my work to Europe, I was so nervous about my inability to speak French that I hired a teacher to help me learn to pronounce the main phrases in my translated statement. It only took a couple of hours, and it was worth it, if only for the unbridled laughter it produced in the French when I attempted to relate what I had learned. Watching me try to discuss complex aesthetic philosophical ideas in a language I didn't understand produced sympathy in my viewers, and soon they were contributing their version of English to the discussion. I made some wonderful new friends.

Using the Internet as a resource. Increasingly, art galleries and museums all over the world are developing Web sites on the Internet. Each site is filled with information about that particular exhibition space and the art it shows. This is a great aid for finding appropriate spaces for your work. To access these Web sites, you will need to get on-line, use any standard search engine (like Infoseek), and type in the city or country you plan to approach, along with words such as *art, museum,* or *gallery*. A long list of possibilities will pop up, and you will need to go through them methodically, which can take some time. Most of these Web sites offer some way of contacting them, usually by E-mail. Why not E-mail the people at the exhibition space, telling them you are an artist planning to visit their city, and asking if they can point you to a gallery guide?

You can also access a newsgroup on-line to ask for information about the art scene in the city you plan to visit. You will get lots of responses, hear lots of opinions and gossip, and probably acquire some valuable inside information as well as making some new friends.

Using the world's biases in your favor. You might be able to skip a few career steps if you remember that the whole world is prejudiced. I'm not talking about racial prejudice; I am talking about location prejudice. No matter where you live, there is always some place more glamorous and another not quite so attractive. The art world has its glamour hierarchies as well. For more than half a century, New York City has been considered the focal point of the art world; before that it was Paris.

Because New York is the center of the art world, Manhattan art professionals sometimes have difficulty taking artists from other parts of the country seriously. The thinking goes something like this: New York is the center of the art world, so if you are serious about being an artist, you should be in New York. Therefore, it follows, that if you are not in New York, you must not be a serious artist. Within the United States itself there are similar hierarchies: Chicago, Los Angeles, and Washington, D.C., follow New York in art status (and any one of them will tell you that the others are not in their league), then the other major cities, followed by small towns everywhere. Status even differs among the small towns. Positioning on either coast is good; being placed in the center of the country is not so good. It's all foolishness, of course, but the biases are there.

New York *is* impressed with Europe, however. And the amazing thing is that Europe welcomes all artists. Of course, if you are from somewhere other than Europe, you are doubly welcome. The first time I took my art to Europe, even though I was a thoroughly unknown artist, apparently unreachable art professionals in France, Germany, Great Britain, and Italy opened their doors to me. This is partly because Europeans hold art in much higher esteem than Americans do, partly because they believe that looking at art by unknown artists is a pivotal part of their job and partly because, to them, non-Europeans seem exotic.

You can use this kind of circular thinking no matter where you live, not only to make things easier for your career, but as an excuse to have an adventure as well. Think about the whole world. Where would you like to go? Japan? Kenya? South America? The farther away from home you go, the more exotic you become. Of course, you can't just go to those places, you have to work, too.

Putting your work on the Internet. The Internet is a truly egalitarian venue for art, and it certainly bypasses the gallery system. Every hour, another artist puts his or her work on-line. It's an exciting new showcase, but what it will really do for the artist is hard to tell. Many artists and galleries are now displaying work for sale on-line, but from the reports I hear, few people are actually buying anything. I've been told that pornographic images are selling, but is anything else? Even if collectors use the Internet to locate art they want to buy, they will probably contact the gallery by phone or by traditional mail. At this point, most people are still afraid to input credit card numbers on the Net; when security problems are ironed out, this may change.

Most of the Internet artists I have spoken with say they are in it for the fun of seeing their art reach so many people at once. It is true that your site may receive thousands of hits a day. But who are these people hitting your site? I suspect that most of them are just surfing by, more interested in the Internet itself than in art.

And then there is the problem of copyright. When you digitize an image, you are making it easy for anyone to steal and use as they wish. You can input it at a low resolution so that it will never look as good as the original, but it still can be lifted. Just out of curiosity, I typed my own name into a search engine on the Internet, and I found my art at four different sites, only one of which I had known about and authorized. The other three were honorable enough to give me credit after they stole my image, otherwise I wouldn't have even known about them. How many others are there who neglected to mention my name?

Even though I distrust the Internet as a marketing tool, I think it is one of the best new tools for artists in terms of research and networking. I've included quite a long list of invaluable sites in the appendix, from the Art Deadlines List, a thorough listing of opportunities for artists, to ArtNet magazine, which presents the latest art issues. Logging-on to some of these terrific sites can stimulate the brain and help remove those isolated artist feelings to which so many of us are prone.

Inventing a new form for showing your art. I can't give you instructions on how to do this since, by definition, a new form hasn't been invented yet. You can use the models described in chapter two as a starting point for ideas. A successful idea will combine at least some of the following characteristics:

- It will differ from the traditional gallery exhibition in some way.
- It will excite your imagination, energy, and passion.
- It will be unusual enough to attract media coverage.
- It will create intellectual dialogue in the art community and, one hopes, in the larger community as well.
- The process and effect of the project will be unpredictable.

Your new form does not have to embody all of these characteristics, but make sure that it includes the element of passion because whatever you invent is certain to involve lots of work. As a strategy for gaining the attention of the art world, an exhibition in an unusual venue can be amazingly effective, but as with everything else, the degree of success will be in proportion to the quality of the work.

Insuring Positive Results

Whichever path or combination of paths you decide upon, there is always an element of risk, because putting your work out there means

> *I prefer the errors of enthusiasm to the indifference of wisdom.*
>
> ANATOLE FRANCE

risking rejection. This is probably the single most common reason that artists don't pursue their careers more actively, and understandably so; rejection hurts.

I can't protect you from rejection, but I can offer some techniques for removing the sting. What we want to achieve is maximum results from our efforts with a minimum of heartbreak.

The first tip. Do your research! (I seem to be repeating myself.) Find out as much as you can about the places you are thinking about approaching, and do not send slides to a gallery if it doesn't handle your kind of work. Even with good research, you can expect only a 10 percent positive response rate.

Some artist consultants counsel a blanket-the-world-with-your-slides approach. I don't recommend it. Not only does this plan incur astronomical slide-duplication and postage costs, it isn't very effective, and it tends to make gallery owners reluctant to open their mail.

> *The notion of making money by popular work, and then retiring to do good work on the proceeds, is the most familiar of all the devil's traps for artists.*
>
> LOGAN PEARSALL SMITH

The second tip. Send out ten to twenty sets of slides at a time (to your targeted list), and as soon as a set is returned, mail it to the next location on your list. That way you don't fixate on any one rejection. You also increase the odds that something good will happen so you can fixate on that.

Tip number three. Think of your goal as collecting rejection slips. The more you get, the more successful you are. If you set a goal of collecting a hundred rejection slips, and you've done your research, then you will probably have to put up with at least ten acceptances. It's a nasty job, but somebody has to do it.

Interpreting a Rejection Slip

A whole book could be written on this topic. There are so many styles and degrees of rejection it boggles the mind. Most galleries have several versions of rejection slips stored on their computers that they modify slightly for each response. Here are some general categories:

The definite rejection. You can tell that you have received a never-darken-our-doors-again rejection if you get a form letter that says something like, "Thank you for sending your slides. We receive so many inquiries that we can't possibly handle them all. Good luck with your career." This translates to "Don't bug us again." My advice is not to bug them again, at least until you have a completely new and different body of work. Let them go. Don't torture yourself trying to acquire their good opinion. You are unlikely to do so, and it will only serve to increase your anxiety level.

The conditional rejection. The text of this letter will include phrases like, "We enjoyed seeing your slides but are unable to accept work at this time. Please send us slides of new work next year." This is really a not-so-bad rejection. What it means is, they liked the work, but they don't think you are ready yet. They want to watch you over time to see how your work develops. This is a common practice. Galleries are often reluctant to invest in an artist until they are convinced of his or her commitment or until the work reaches a mature level, so they ask the artist to keep them posted. In your next cover letter, you can say, "Thank you so much for your warm response to my work last year. Here are some new slides as you requested." That way they will be reminded that they want to see the work, just in case they forgot.

The rejection that is really an acceptance (without the tedious bother of actually getting a show). This type of rejection is, of course, my favorite. These letters are not form letters. They are written in obvious response to seeing and liking the work. Sometimes the writers will go on at length about how wonderful your art is, but then finish with some reason why they can't act on their feelings. The reason could be that they are booked for two years, or that they love your work but they just know their clients won't go for it, or that it is too big for their space. A letter like this is a treasure, because it means that you have made a connection. Write them back immediately and thank them for

I think all great innovations are built on rejections.
LOUISE NEVELSON

their thoughtful response to your work. Tell them you are saddened that they can't work with you, but that you understand. Ask them if they have any suggestions for other venues for the work. Don't be a pest, but keep the doors of communication open. Send them new slides when you have them. Keep it friendly, and eventually it may turn into something.

The Acceptance Letter

Eventually you will get one, then more than one, acceptance letter. You will be able to recognize it right away, without any coaching. My advice is to go out and celebrate.

Tomorrow the real work begins.

CHAPTER FIVE

When Things Begin to Happen

"At your opening, I see that you had two glasses of wine, eight pieces of cheddar, eight crackers, and seventeen grapes. That, of course, will have to come off the top of your end."

Once people begin to be interested in your work, you will start participating in a whole new set of activities. You will form new relationships with a variety of art professionals, learn to deal with contracts and consignment forms, make framing decisions, ship your art, manage deadlines, and deal with sales. This can be a very exciting time, and a confusing one; the adventure has begun. This is what you wanted to happen, remember?

A useful rule of thumb when entering this new arena is: When in doubt, ask. Most of the problems that arise between artists and galleries occur because each participant makes different assumptions about the nature of the relationship. Don't be afraid of sounding like a beginner. Everyone is a beginner at one time or another, so why not take the opportunity to ask lots of questions. It is the quickest way to learn about the business and about the people you are dealing with as well.

My personal strategy is to ask the dumbest question I can think of right away. After that, I can't be afraid of ruining my image. I know this won't work for everyone, but it gives me a tremendous sense of freedom, and I find it interesting to watch the effect on the person I am dealing with. If they respond with kindness and patience, the relationship will probably be a good one; if they are condescending and abrupt, I know I will have to be on my toes in dealing with them.

> *Genius can probably run on ahead and seek out new ways. But the good artists who follow after genius—and I count myself among these—have to restore the lost connection once more.*
>
> KÄTHE KOLLWITZ

Once You Have Been Invited to Participate in an Exhibition

An invitation to participate in an exhibition is not the same as being invited to join a gallery; it is more like a one-night stand that lasts about a month. Over the length of your career, you will hang your art in hundreds, maybe thousands, of one-shot exhibitions, in many different kinds and sizes of exhibition spaces. Adopting a policy of communication at the start of your career will save you hours of frustration. There are specific issues you will want to discuss with the curator of each show.

Date and location of the exhibition. You need to know the opening and closing dates of the show, the reception date and hours, the due date for delivery of the art, and the date for the return of the art.

How many pieces will be included in the exhibition and/or how much space will be available for your work? If this is a juried show, the gallery will have already chosen which pieces are to be admitted into the exhibition. If it is an invitational or a several-person show, the curator will probably want to choose the specific works to be shown, either by making a visit to your studio or from viewing slides of the work. For a one-person show, the artist usually has more control. If you can, visit the exhibition space before the show and talk to the curator about it. It will help you anticipate and forestall potential difficulties.

Who is responsible for framing the art? The answer will probably be that you are. If the expense of framing the show will be difficult for you, ask the gallery if it has any suggestions for cutting the cost; perhaps it is willing to hang the show unframed, under glass. Or maybe it will frame your work for you and take the cost out of your first sales. There is always the chance that the gallery will agree to share the cost with you; it can't hurt to ask.

Who is responsible for hanging the show? Does the gallery employ a staff for the installation of its exhibitions, or will you be expected to hang the show yourself? If the staff is installing the show, how much input do they expect from the artist? Artists, especially at the beginning of their careers, are often nervous about hanging a show and tend to feel an urgent need to be in control of every aspect of the hanging. It is a good idea to give some attention to this matter, just long enough to ascertain that the curator is handling the work with care and sequencing the show with intelligence and attention. Beyond that, I have found that it is best to step back and allow the curator to do his or her job. As a professional, a talented curator can bring out the strength in your work in ways you may not have imagined. Ordinarily, the only time you will need to participate in the hanging is if a piece involves a particularly tricky installation; even then, give the curator plenty of room for input. You will probably be pleasantly surprised.

If the work needs to be shipped. Who will pay the shipping costs, and how is the art to be shipped? Standard practice is for the artist to pay

> *We moan about not working; and if we get a job we moan about the director, the script, and the reviews. If the play's a hit, we moan about the long run ahead of us. Then we moan because the play closes and we're out of work.*
>
> DEREK JACOBI

the cost of shipping the art to the show, with the gallery absorbing the return cost. The exceptions to this rule are juried shows, which often demand that the artist pay for shipping both ways. If it is a museum show, the museum usually pays for the shipping.

Exhibition announcements. Most exhibitions are accompanied by an announcement stating the date and location of the show, and the reception date, if there is one. For group and juried shows, the announcement usually lists the participants but does not carry a picture on the front. For one- or two-person shows, a reproduction of a work of art will often be added. You will want to find out if the announcement will be printed in color or black and white, and whether or not a photo of your work will appear. Full-color announcements used to be the norm, but today, with gallery cutbacks, almost anything goes. If the gallery won't pay for a color announcement and you can afford it, you might offer to share the cost of color printing. Since the announcement will reach many more people than will actually be able to attend the show, a reproduction of your strongest piece can give them a taste of the experience. In addition, full-color cards with nice reproductions can be used long beyond the time frame of the show. Ask the gallery director to print some extras for your use later on. The gallery will usually agree to give you a hundred or so extra announcements without charge; very many more may mean additional "run-on" costs.

Mailing list. How large is the gallery mailing list, and who is on it? Is the gallery willing to pay postage for your mailing list as well? Usually it will assume the cost for at least part of your list; find out how many announcements have been allotted to you. Does the gallery want your list supplied on labels or on disk? When do they need it?

Will there be a reception? Most shows have them. You will want to know the date and time for the reception, who will pay for it, and what will be served. Usually the gallery absorbs the cost of the reception, although today it is seldom more elaborate than wine and mineral water, with maybe some grapes or cheese thrown in.

As an artist you have to be a thief and steal a place on the rich man's wall.

MARK ROTHKO

Publicity. What kind of advertising will the gallery do? If it plans on mailing a press release, will it provide the promotional photographs or will you? When will the press release be mailed? Does the gallery have any special relationships with local critics? Is there any way you can help with this? There is a lot of give and take in this area. Each gallery has its own way of doing things, but usually it is thrilled if you are willing to take some responsibility for arranging publicity. Sometimes you may have to take the initiative entirely, but that is worth the extra work.

Insurance. Will the work be insured by the gallery? Most established galleries do insure artwork against damage, fire, and theft. If the show is in a café, or other space not normally used for exhibiting art, they may not. If not, you will need to decide whether or not you want to assume that responsibility. Insurance costs are very high, so you will have to weigh that against your ability to replace the art should something happen to it. Call your insurance company and ask about costs.

Gallery commission. When the work is sold, what percentage of the retail price will the gallery take? (This could range from zero to 50 percent.) How soon can you expect to be paid?

After the show. If the show is at a nonprofit space, alternative space, or museum, the gallery staff will expect you to remove the work as soon as the show comes down to make room for the next exhibit. If it is at a commercial gallery, they may want to keep some work on hand for a while to show to their clients, or they may want you to join the gallery.

Issues to Discuss with a Gallery that Wants to Handle Your Work

At last, a gallery is willing to take a chance on you. This is, you hope, the beginning of a long and happy relationship. Start it right by taking the responsibility for opening up the communication channels. Topics for discussion should include, but not be limited to, the following.

The nature of the relationship. It used to be that when a dealer invited an artist to join the gallery, it indicated a commitment to stand by that artist throughout his or her career. Today there are many variations on the theme. The gallery may want to try the work out for one show, checking the clients' reactions before making a more permanent arrangement. It may be interested in the art for one exhibition only (maybe it fits the theme of a specific show but not the overall direction of the gallery), or it may want representation rights. If a gallery wants to represent you, you will need to find out if they expect exclusivity or not, and how they define *exclusivity*. Exclusivity means that a gallery expects to be the only place in a given metropolitan area which handles your work; if someone in that area wants to buy your work, they must go to that gallery. Beware of any gallery expecting worldwide rights. Exclusive rights to a specific city is a more reasonable expectation. If a gallery asks for national rights, they must be willing and able to provide work to galleries in other regions for shows and sales. Few galleries have the staff, and connections, to do that.

As ugly as the work is, no work is so ugly that it can't be assimilated.
LEON GOLUB

Which work do they want? Sometimes a gallery will like your paintings but not your drawings. You need to clarify this so that you can find another dealer for your drawings if the first gallery doesn't want them. Sometimes the dealer can suggest a second gallery for the art. This can work to everyone's advantage if it's a happy threesome; but as always, communication is the key. The two galleries can use their double clout to promote the work, and you will be able to have all your work seen.

Find out how many pieces the gallery intends to keep on hand between shows. Will it want to keep the work indefinitely or send it back after a certain number of months? Does the gallery expect to receive the work from you matted and framed, or will they assume that responsibility? Who will pay for shipping? What insurance coverage is provided? What is the policy on consigning work to other galleries? You will want to have a say in this, since otherwise the gallery can ship your work off to Mars without your knowing it.

How often can you expect to be given a solo show? Depending on the number of artists a gallery represents, an artist should expect to hang a show of new work every two years; sometimes less, sometimes more. There are many factors determining this, such as how many artists the gallery is prepared to handle and, of course, your own output as an artist. There is a wonderful painter, Katherine Huffaker Jones, who works in the studio every day and manages to turn out about three paintings a year. She makes marvelous eight-by-ten-foot paintings with a tiny triple-zero brush. The work is so meticulous it takes her months to complete one piece. Obviously, she won't be ready for a show of new work every two years; six paintings do not fill a gallery. Other artists work very quickly and can fill a gallery every couple of months. If the gallery director thinks the work will sell, he or she is likely to arrange shows more frequently. Then again, the gallery may lean more toward group shows than solo shows. Ask what the policy is, and try to get at least a tentative commitment to dates for a solo show of your work. The dates may be changed later, but at least you will have a point to start from.

Being an artist is like walking a tightrope. All those little temptations are waiting underneath. The moment you try to please a dealer or make a couch painting, you've sold a little bit of yourself. You can never get back to the tightrope.

DOROTHY GILLESPIE

Is the gallery willing to sign a written contract with you? Dealers often balk at this. They cite reasons such as "the need for trust" and the relationship is "like a marriage," but I suspect that they are opposed to contracts because, without a contract, all the power lies in the hands of the dealers. Twenty years ago nobody offered artist-gallery contracts, but, thankfully, the practice is becoming increasingly frequent. If the gallery has a standard contract, don't just sign it; you will probably be giving away more rights than you want to. Ask a lawyer to review it and make the changes you need. Don't just show it to any lawyer, you need one who specializes in business law. You can find one, usually with a sliding pay scale to accommodate a limited income, through your state's Lawyers for the Arts organization (see appendix). Once you have consulted a lawyer, discuss the contract again with the dealer. A standard contract is just a starting point. No one expects it to be signed without some discussion and changes. If the gallery doesn't have a standard contract, then use one that benefits you. I have included a copy of a contract written by the California Lawyers for the Arts in the appendix. It seems to cover most of the important points.

A friendly way to institute a contract with your dealer was suggested to me by an art dealer in Washington, D.C. Let the contract develop organically, as the natural outcome of your discussions with your dealer. After you have talked with the dealer and discussed all the salient points regarding your relationship, have a lawyer draw up a contract tailored to fit the facts. The result should be a contract that meets the needs of both parties. If the dealer is reluctant to sign it, then consider carefully whether or not you want to get involved with this person. A dealer who is not willing to sign a paper that basically restates what has already been agreed to may not be willing to honor that verbal agreement in the future.

A contract won't protect you from crooks, but it will help avoid misunderstandings between yourself and honorable dealers. A contract will also protect you in the legal arena, should a misunderstanding ever go that far.

In the art world, you can't be right all the time, but you can never be wrong.
DAVE HICKEY

What are the gallery's responsibilities beyond the exhibition? What will the gallery do to promote sales and attract attention to your work? Does it have a strategy for promoting your art career? Does it have connections with collectors, critics, and curators to use on your behalf? Convey the idea that you will be expecting a dealer to take an active roll in promoting your career, and that you are willing to do your part in turn.

What does the gallery expect of you in return? Mostly it will expect you to continue to make incredible art; that's why they were interested in you in the first place. Beyond that, it will want you to behave in a professional manner, to meet your commitments on time, to be willing to meet with collectors when asked to, and to treat your dealers honorably.

VARA: Moral Rights in Your Art

What are moral rights in art? Artists' moral rights have been recognized in Europe under the term *droit moral*. These are rights that the artist retains in his or her work even after its sale and that remain with the artist regardless of who owns the copyright. The rights are separate from the economic rights protected under the Copyright Act.

What rights are "moral rights"? Moral rights are the rights of the artist to be able to claim or disclaim authorship in a work (Right of Attribution) and to maintain the integrity of his or her work of art (Right of Integrity).

How are they protected? Congress passed a law called the Visual Artists Rights Act (VARA) that amended the Copyright Act of 1976; it became effective June 1, 1991.

What does VARA do? VARA establishes a single federal standard regarding artists' rights to be applied to art created in the United States. It defines the term "work of visual art" and describes in detail the Right of Attribution and Right of Integrity.

A Work of Visual Art. Essentially, a work of art is:
- A painting, drawing, sculpture, print, or still photographic image produced for exhibition purposes only and existing in a single copy;
- A print in a limited edition of 200 or less, all signed and numbered consecutively;
- A sculpture produced in a multiple of 200 or less, all numbered and having the sculptor's name or mark; and
- A still photographic image produced for exhibition purposes only in a limited edition of 200 or less, all signed and numbered consecutively.

The Right of Attribution. The "Right of Attribution" is the right to claim or disclaim authorship of a work of art. This allows you to disclaim authorship if your work of art is mutilated or modified in such a way that it would harm your reputation as an artist to retain authorship of the work.

The Right of Integrity: The "Right of Integrity" is the right to preserve the integrity of your work of art against intentional destruction, mutilation or other modification that would harm your reputation, and to prevent the intentional or grossly negligent destruction of a work of "recognized stature." The exceptions to this right are damage or mutilation caused by the passage of time or inherent in the nature of the materials used and damage or modification due to conservation or exhibition, unless caused by gross negligence.

How long do these rights last? These rights last for the life of the artist for works created after June 1, 1991 (the effective date of VARA). For works created before June 1, 1991, VARA does not apply unless the work was not transferred until after that date. If VARA does not apply, you may be covered under state law if you live in a state that has a law governing artists' rights. These states include California, Connecticut, Georgia, Louisiana, Maine, Montana, Massachusetts, Nevada, New Jersey, New York, Pennsylvania, Rhode Island, and Utah.

State law or federal law? VARA, which is a federal law, has precedence over (preempts, in legal language) state law. This means that its provisions control any issue. However, if state law grants more rights—for example, the rights last longer under state law, as in California—the greater state rights are not preempted and will apply.

What are the remedies if the rights are violated? VARA does not provide for any specific remedies, but because VARA is an amendment to the Copyright Act, the civil remedies under that Act apply. There are no criminal penalties.

Can the rights be transferred? The rights cannot be transferred, but they can be waived if the artist prepares and signs a written document expressly stating the right(s) being waived and the specific work is identified.

Do I have to do anything to have these rights? No. Just create your work of art, as defined in the law.

Copyright: Legal Protection for your Art

What is copyright? Copyright is legal protection under federal law to "authors" (that's you) of "original works of authorship" (that's your photograph, painting, sculpture, or other type of original work).

The common misconception. Most people think that they have to put the copyright notice on their work in order to be protected. In fact, you have protection as soon as you start to make your work and it becomes "fixed in a tangible form of expression." However, if you register your copyright with the Copyright Office, you will be able to take advantage of the greater legal rights and remedies provided under the law.

Protection from what? For visual artists, copyright protection provides you with the exclusive right to do and authorize others to do the following:

- Reproduce your work;
- Prepare derivative work;
- Distribute copies of your work by sale, rental, or otherwise;
- Display the copyrighted work publicly.

Anyone other than the copyright owner who does any of these things without permission of the copyright owner is in violation of the law and is subject to civil and, in some rare cases, criminal penalties.

What is protected? Copyright protects the form of an idea, but not the idea. For example, you can't protect the idea of a cat, but you can protect your painting, photograph, or sculpture of a cat. Names, titles, and slogans are not protected.

When is a work covered by copyright? Copyright exists as soon as the original work becomes "fixed in a tangible form of expression" which can be seen without or with the aid of a machine or device (as a film). Copyright law requires that the work have a minimal amount of creativity and originality. In order to obtain maximum protection, it is necessary to register your copyright with the Copyright Office of the Library of Congress.

Who is the owner of the copyright? The "author" of the work is the owner of the copyright, not the current owner of the work itself (no matter whether ownership was transferred by sale, gift, or otherwise), unless the author has transferred, in a signed, written document, one or more rights under the copyright. The only exception is work produced by an employee or "for hire." In that case the employer owns the copyright.

How long does copyright protection last? For the life of the "author" plus fifty years.

How is copyright indicated on a work? The copyright indication is called the copyright notice. It is not required, and failure to use it does not result in loss of protection. Lawyers will advise you to use the notice, but many people in the art world feel that it cheapens the work. Registering the work with the copyright office should be sufficient. Use the copyright symbol on your slides, however. Proper copyright notice contains three parts:

- The copyright symbol ©;
- The year of first publication (the distribution of copies of the work to the public by sale or other transfer; display of work not for sale does not constitute publication);
- The name of owner of copyright in the work (that is, you, the artist/author).

Proper notice will look like this: ©1997 Penelope Painter

The notice needs to be placed so it will give "reasonable notice" that the work is covered by copyright and be "permanently affixed" to the work.

How is a copyright registered? First, you do not need a lawyer. To register a copyright with the Copyright Office of the Library of Congress, you send them the following three things in the same envelope:

- An application form, properly completed (Form VA, for published and unpublished works of the visual arts);
- A check for $20 for each application;
- A deposit of the work being registered (actually a copy of the original work).

After your application has been reviewed, you will receive a Certificate of Registration of Copyright. That's it. You are fully covered.

How do I get more information? Detailed instructions on all aspects of copyright can be obtained from the Copyright Office by writing to:

Registrar of Copyrights
Library of Congress
Washington, D.C. 20559

Or you can call the Hotline at 202-707-3000. To order forms, call 202-707-9100. Information is also available on the Internet at:

World Wide Web URL: http://lcweb.loc.gov/copyright
Gopher: marvel.loc.gov, port 70
Telnet: marvel.loc.gov and login as marvel

The Copyright Office publishes a wide variety of circulars in simple, nontechnical language that explain all you need to know about copyright protection and registration. The best place to start is with Circular 1, Copyright Basics. Circular 2, Publications on Copyright, lists all the items published by the Copyright Office that will help you understand the details of what you have to do to get the maximum protection available for your work.

What is the Resale Royalty Right? European moral rights also include the right of the artist to receive a payment each time a work is resold (sometimes only if at a greater value). The royalty right is similar to the royalties paid to songwriters, playwrights, and authors of literature, and is generally based on the idea that the artist should benefit from the increased value of his or her work of art that has resulted from the artist's increased reputation as he or she continues to produce work.

Is the Resale Royalty Right available in the United States? A section of VARA required a study and recommendation regarding the implementation of such a right in the United States. However, no federal legislation has been passed or even proposed to date because of opposition to its concept by some famous artists and others. This opposition is based, in part, on the fear that it would make it more difficult to sell work because the price would have to be higher to cover the royalty, and that it would depress the value of unknown artists' work because buyers would think that the artist would receive additional compensation on later sales.

California, the lone exception. There is one exception to the absence of resale royalty rights in the United States. In 1976, California passed the Resale Royalty Act, which entitles the artist to 5 percent of the resale price if the resale price is greater than the purchase price.

What to Expect when
Working with a Dealer

The higher the status the gallery holds in the art community, the more professional you can expect them to be in their dealings with you. In addition, the higher your status is as an artist (the more well-known), the more you can expect the gallery to do for you. For example, if you are just beginning your career, the gallery will probably expect you to bear the expense of framing your work. If you are more established, the gallery will assume that responsibility. The gallery's willingness to accept extra obligations is in direct proportion to the amount of money or degree of prestige they expect to gain from showing your work. This means that, regardless of the gallery's stated policy in dealing with artists, they may be open to making special arrangements depending on the situation.

Thanks to art, instead of seeing a single world, our own, we see it multiply until we have before us as many worlds as there are original artists.

MARCEL PROUST

Artists usually change galleries several times during their careers; the successful ones negotiate a more favorable arrangement with each move. This highlights the importance of learning to negotiate. Almost every artist I have met shows a reluctance to negotiate, either by natural inclination or because their upbringing did not prepare them for it. I am one of those artists. For years, I meekly took the first thing people offered me because I felt uncomfortable asking for more. I was afraid I would have to become the kind of person I dislike, manipulative and argumentative.

If you never ask for what you want, however, you will never get it. I decided to make an experiment out of learning to negotiate. I wanted to see if I could get what I desired simply by asking for it. The next time I needed to discuss an upcoming exhibit with my dealer, I drew up a chart and took it with me. In the first column I listed all the things I wanted, in the second column what the gallery was offering; I left the third column open for writing down our compromise. When I sat down to talk with the director, I went over my list and asked for each item in turn. I didn't coerce; I didn't threaten; I didn't manipulate; I didn't get all agitated. I just asked. I figured that if they said no to everything I wanted, I would not have lost anything anyway. To my surprise, the gallery was happy to give me quite a few of the things I was asking for. With the other issues, I found that by discussing them with my dealer I learned more about how the gallery made decisions and planted the seeds for further discussion.

This is a pain-free, unbelievably easy, and morally clean method for taking care of yourself. It also sets the tone for your relationship with the gallery in the future. This approach creates a professional atmosphere, one of honest agendas and mutual giving and taking. As your relationship with your dealer deepens, you will begin to know each other and eventually trust that you are working together for the same end. If the relationship does not advance, you will be able to pinpoint where the problems lie.

For this trust to develop, you will need to be scrupulously honest and responsible in all your dealings with the gallery. This means meeting your deadlines on time; keeping the gallery up-to-date on your latest work; providing them with whatever slides, bios, or other materials they need to do their job, and never selling work behind their back or undercutting their prices. This doesn't mean that you can't sell work out of your studio; it just means that you need to have an understanding with your gallery about it beforehand. Most galleries don't mind if you sell work yourself, they just don't want to be cut out of the loop.

Protecting Yourself

Writing a follow-up letter. After you have come to an agreement with the gallery or exhibition director about your mutual expectations and responsibilities, write a follow-up letter describing your understanding of the discussion and mail it right away. The purpose is to prevent misunderstandings later on and also to serve as proof of your agreement in a court of law if necessary. The letter may say something like, *"Dear Fred: I am thrilled to be showing my work at your gallery during the month of July in 1999. My understanding is that my responsibilities include: (fill it in). You will be responsible for: (fill it in). If there is any error in my understanding of our arrangement, please let me know."*

Be fastidious in keeping a written record of all your gallery-related correspondence, phone conversations, and meetings. Whenever you talk with someone on the phone, write down the gist of the conversation, date it, and put it in your files. Write a follow-up letter after every conversation, in person or on the phone, summarizing your understanding of the subjects covered in the discussion. If the gallery has a different understanding, it will let you know. You will then be able to clarify any points about which you disagree.

Writing a consignment agreement. One of the best ways to protect yourself and keep a record of your art at the same time is to use a consignment form that contains (in small print) all the main points you would have put in a contract. I have included a copy of the one I use in chapter six. Dealers who object to signing contracts will often sign consignment forms without question, since they do it all the time. Always fill out a consignment form whenever your art leaves your studio, even if the gallery has a form of its own. It helps keep track of your art and assures you that the person you consigned the work to has agreed to your terms. Of course, it is useless if it is not signed, so always make two copies, one for the gallery and one for you, and get both signed when you deliver the art.

I don't advise anyone to take it [painting] up as a business proposition,
unless they really have talent, and are crippled so as to deprive them
of physical labor. Then, with help, they might make a living.

GRANDMA MOSES

CHAPTER SIX

Creating Your Command Post

Your office is the hub of your professional activities, the center point from which you enter the world as an artist. You will want it to be well organized and easy to work in, with all the procedures streamlined. The easier it is to work in your office, the less time you will spend there. That means more time for making art.

The ideal office includes a desk with filing cabinets, a computer, a printer, a telephone, and a comfortable chair, all preferably in a separate room. If setting up a private office is impossible for you right now, start with what is possible. Most office supply stores sell portable filing boxes with handles that are easy to transport and perfect for keeping all of your materials in one place. Make the filing box your command center. If you don't have a computer, borrow a friend's or use one at a local copy shop for an hourly rate. Carry your portable office and a floppy disk containing your standard letters and mailing list with you, and you can become fully functional in minutes at any borrowed or rented computer station. If you don't know how to use a computer and don't want to learn, you can find an enthusiastic and inexpensive work force at any university or junior college near you. College students understand how to use computers, and they always need work.

If being organized comes naturally to you, count yourself lucky. To you nonmethodical types, I'm sorry, but I don't see any way around it. Perhaps you can talk your beloved into doing this for you. Try pleading, "I'm just a flaky artist. I need someone more grounded, *like you*, to help me." Or maybe, "I am a genius. I only deal with the larger issues."

Actually, some of the most successful artists have had just such an arrangement with their spouses. The artist makes the art and their partner handles the business. This can be heavenly if the partner believes wholeheartedly in your art and enjoys being a part of the experience. He or she will need to have the time to attend to your career on a regular basis, an affinity for business, and a policy of noninterference when it comes to the art-making itself. The last thing you need is someone else telling you what to paint.

Another plan is to hire someone to oversee your business for you. My first office assistants came from a local university. I hired them for one to two days a week at an embarrassingly low rate. Some of them were wonderful, knowledgeable, organized, and energetic; others were less than ideal. I always ask new assistants to make a commitment for a minimum of six months, because it takes that long to become familiar with the job. Even if someone else is running the office, you will still need to supervise everything they do, at least until you are secure in the knowledge that you and your assistant are on the same planet. I once had an assistant who filed everything under secret code names in honor of her stuffed animals to make the job "more in-

Genius begins great works; labor alone finishes them.

JOSEPH JOUBERT

teresting." I didn't discover this until I tried to find a gallery file while she was on vacation in Mexico. It was not my best day.

Make a habit of keeping clear and accurate records of everything that you do. This means producing a copy for your files of every letter and show application you send out and writing confirming letters after each phone call, as well as retaining notes from all your conversations. Set up your office so that creating a paper trail is easy, otherwise you won't remember where your slides are, how to get them back, or what you promised to whom. If you don't keep good records, you run the risk of losing a lot of those not-so-cheap slides, messing up on making your contact calls, misplacing your art, and screwing up your relationships with those dealers you worked so hard to get.

I arise in the morning torn between a desire to save the world and a desire to savor the world. That makes it hard to plan the day.

E. B. WHITE

The miraculous computer. Aren't computers amazing? It may take a while to get them installed, but when they are running smoothly, they can streamline your work so that it actually becomes pleasurable.

Once you have access to a computer, you will want to create some basic materials that you can standardize and use repeatedly with minor changes. These materials should include a stationery and envelope template (unless you have preprinted stationery), a standard cover letter for sending out slides, your bio, your artist statements, labels for your slides, and a mailing list. You can create most of these documents in a standard word-processing program like WordPerfect or Microsoft Word. The exception is the mailing list, which will need to be created in a database program like Filemaker. You can also buy programs specifically designed for maintaining mailing lists, such as Bulk Mailer. A wonderful set of programs that combines a tracking system for your business activities with a mailing list and a well-organized calendar is Now Contact and Now Up-To-Date. The two usually are sold together, and in some cases they arrive already installed on your computer. I have recently switched everything to these programs, except for word processing and stationery design. Now Contact will even dial the phone for you, if you have a modem, *and* keep track of your calls!

If you are using someone else's computer, you won't have to bother buying any of these programs. Just use the word-processing program already installed and store all your standard information on a floppy disk which you keep in your portable file. It is a good idea to make a back-up disk as well, just in case anything should happen to the materials on the first one. Store the back-up disk in another location.

A filing system. Keep your filing system simple and direct. The idea is to be able to find what you are looking for without a lot of effort. Standard file-folder titles can include terms such as Artist Bio, Artist Statement, Art Consultants, Art Dealers, Consignments, Donations, Exhibitions, Inventory List, Invoices, Juried Shows, Publications, Slide Masters (for keeping), Slide Duplicates (for circulating), Slides Out List, Plans, Goals, and Leads. Pick the categories that apply to you, adding to the list as necessary.

Keeping Records of Your Activities

As a successful artist, you will be participating in numerous activities that may not be art but are essential to your career nonetheless, such as sending out slides for consideration, shipping artwork to and from exhibitions, and consigning works to galleries. You will need to keep track of all this. The best way to do this is to set up a simple, yet thorough, method for dealing with each activity. For sending out slides and other promotional materials, I use a Slides Out List; for keeping track of the location of my artwork, I use an Inventory List, and for consigning artwork to galleries I use a Consignment Form.

Most artists are forced to act as their own patrons.

JIM MELCHERT

The slides out list. I became acquainted with the use of the Slides Out List when I took a job as an assistant to art dealer Yancey Richardson several years back. I don't know whether the Slides Out List is her creation, but she used it whenever she sent out any promotional materials, whether they were slides, glossies, 4" x 5" transparencies, or written materials; anything but the actual art. It quickly became apparent why, because it is amazingly easy to forget important details. The Slides Out List can remind you with the minimum amount of effort on your part. I have included a copy of my own Slides Out List. Lift it and use it as it is, or create your own, using mine as a guideline.

The form is self explanatory. Fill out each section completely, especially the name, address, and phone number, even when you are in

Slides Out List

Date	Name and Address	Phone	Inclusions	Follow-up	Return date
			slides 4" x 5" glossies bio statement SASE other		
			slides 4" x 5" glossies bio statement SASE other		
			slides 4" x 5" glossies bio statement SASE other		
			slides 4" x 5" glossies bio statement SASE other		
			slides 4" x 5" glossies bio statement SASE other		

a hurry. Whenever I don't write down all the information, I always regret it. Six months later I will be reviewing the list, come across some name like Elroy Zruchisican, and not be able to remember who he is or where he lives or why I sent slides to him in the first place. If I haven't written in his address or phone number I find it difficult to do my follow-up calls, obviously, and impossible to retrieve my slides.

In the Inclusions column, I circle the type of materials sent—slides, glossies, 4" x 5"s or a combination—so that I don't have to keep writing the same information over and over. I also list the exact images sent. This can be helpful when your slide packet is returned with one slide missing, which is a fairly frequent occurrence. Often a gallery will keep one or two slides in case they have a use for them later on. I find it especially frustrating not knowing which ones; it's just a minor irritation, but you can avoid it by planning ahead.

The Follow-up column is where you list your follow-up phone calls as you make them, and specific comments or requests made by the gallery. Use it as a reminder column, so you know what to do next. In the return column, I write in the date the slides were returned.

Keeping inventory. If you are even remotely prolific as an artist, it will soon become apparent that you are going to need some sort of tracking device to monitor the location of your artwork at any given moment. Most artists use an Inventory List, which differs from the Slides Out List in that it keeps track of actual art rather than promotional materials.

The secret to having a useful inventory list is to use it faithfully every time a piece of art leaves your studio, whether it is for an exhibition, on consignment to a gallery, or as a sale. If you are haphazard about posting this information, the inventory list will soon become meaningless.

I am including two versions of the Inventory List. The first one is for artists who make one-of-a-kind pieces; the second is for multiples.

If you make multiple images, such as photographs or prints, or if your work is constantly moving in and out of your studio for one reason or another, I recommend creating an inventory list with an entire page devoted to the activities of each piece.

This type of inventory list can be kept in one of your file folders, or

A functional artist should have five shows waiting in the wings.

DOROTHY GILLESPIE

if you have lots of images, in a loose-leaf notebook. If you really want to be thorough, copy a small photograph of the piece and glue it to the upper right corner of the inventory sheet. That way, someone other than yourself who is trying to locate a piece won't have to memorize the names of all your artwork; there will be a visual clue to help them.

The Consignment Form. I love my Consignment Form. It has saved me every time I have experienced any trouble over lost or damaged art work. Once it even came to my rescue when a disreputable gallery owner tried to involve me in tax evasion and an insurance scam. This dealer had held over twenty of my photographs on consignment for some time, and had neither sold nor returned them. One evening, at a dinner party, a colleague mentioned that several of my pieces had been donated by the dealer to a local museum (obviously as a tax write-off). I was furious. The dealer didn't own that work. When I called her to ask for payment, she said I must be mistaken since all my photographs had been destroyed when her house burned down. "Wouldn't you rather have the insurance money?" she purred. All I had to do was falsify my copies of the consignment forms and send them to her. Since I knew for certain that at least some of the photographs had survived the fire, it was clear she wanted to involve me in fraud. I refused and pointed out that the works were in perfect condition when she received them because she had signed a consignment form to that effect. I told her I expected payment from her and that I would turn this matter over to my lawyer. Eventually we settled out of court. I ended up with less than was owed me (mostly because I didn't have the stomach for a long court battle), but if it hadn't been for my lovely Consignment Form, I would have ended up with nothing.

Use a Consignment Form every time you ship or hand-deliver art work for an exhibition, or to a gallery or art consultant who will be selling or showing the work. The only time you don't need one is when you are selling the art directly to a client. If they are buying it, then obviously it is not on loan.

When you fill out the form, be sure to fill in all the blanks: your name, their name and address, and the period of consignment. If you are consigning the work to a gallery, it generally will want the work for a period of three to six months, but discuss the time period with

I've handled color as a man should behave. You may conclude that I consider ethics and aesthetics as one.

JOSEF ALBERS

Inventory List

(for one-of-a-kind pieces)

Disposition Code: S=Sale; D=Donation; R=Rental; C=Consignment; L=Loan; E=Exhibition

Date	Title	Disposition	Name, Address, Phone	Return Date

Inventory List

(for multiples or artwork that is shown a lot)

Title of piece:

Date created:

Materials:

Negative number (if applicable):

Size of piece:

Size of edition:

Disposition Code: S=Sale; D=Donation; R=Rental; C=Consignment; L=Loan; E=Exhibition

Print #	Disposition	Date out	Name, address, phone	Return date	If sold, to whom?

Works on Consignment Agreement

This agreement dated _____ is between _____, the artist, and _____, the consignee, located at _____. The consignee accepts on consignment for a period of _____ days the following artworks:

Title & Edition	Description	Size	Condition	Retail Price	Comments

The works are on loan only. The artist retains copyright and full ownership of the artworks. In the event of a sale of an artwork, the artist will be paid _____% (percent) of the retail price within thirty days of the purchase. Works not sold within the agreed time will be returned to the artist in the condition received. The consignee is responsible for the full value of all works damaged while in his/her possession or due to inadequate handling or shipping materials and procedures. Works are to be insured by the consignee while in his/her possession.

Signed, _____, artist, and _____, consignee.

the owner. If, at the end of that time, the gallery would like to keep the work longer, the consignment form will still be valid, as long as you agree. If you want the work back, the consignment form will support your wishes.

In filling out the chart, be very specific about the condition of the work. Since I make photographic prints, I always list the edition number so that the client and I know exactly which photograph we are talking about. If the photograph is newly printed and has not been touched by human hands (other than the printer), I write "new" in the condition column. If it has been around a while and is still in perfect condition, I write "good" or "perfect." I never send out work that is not in good condition. If there is a minor flaw, such as a bent corner, I mention it in the comments column. The comments column may also be used to insert extra information, such as whether the work is matted or framed.

The retail price is the price the work will sell for, not what you will get paid. Down in the small print at the bottom you will see a _____% space. Be sure to fill that out. With a commercial gallery, it will usually be 50 percent, but sometimes the arrangement will be different. If your agreement is 60-40, with you getting the 60 percent, be sure that you write 60, not 40, in the blank.

Make three copies of the consignment form. One for you, one for the consignee, and a third for your files in case the others get lost. Deliver two copies with your signature to the gallery along with the artwork, requesting that the recipient sign them both and return one for your files. It's a good idea to enclose a stamped, self-addressed envelope to make it easy for them to comply.

Upon receipt of the work, the gallery staff will inspect the art to make certain it is in good condition. Sometimes they find something wrong that you didn't see, which immediately makes filling out a consignment form worth the trouble. A problem has been solved before it has become a problem. The gallery director will pick up the telephone and mention that, for instance, there is a fingerprint in the lower right hand corner. If it is a small thing, suggest that they make a note of it on the consignment form before they sign it. If there is a major problem with the work, ask them to return it for replacement.

The superior man understands what is right; the inferior man understands what will sell.

CONFUCIUS

Dealing with Pricing and Sales

Making pricing decisions. There are two ways to price your work. The first method, which I don't recommend, is to decide the amount you want to be paid (the wholesale price), and then let your various dealers add whatever they want when selling to their clients. The second approach is to set a selling price (the retail price), and decide in conjunction with each dealer or client the amount of commission they will receive from the sale of the work. If it is a commercial gallery it will probably be 50 percent, which means you will only receive half of the retail price, so set your prices accordingly.

The advantage to the second pricing method lies in the fact that your prices will be consistent across the globe. This is worth considering. You don't want a client who bought a photograph for $2,500 from your New York gallery to discover that it could have been purchased for $2,000 in Los Angeles. The art world is very small; people talk with each other on the phone every day (that is how international galleries do business), and they do find out these things. You run the risk of appearing unprofessional, and worse, it brings into question the intrinsic value of your work.

There are several factors to consider when pricing your work, and this requires that you juggle all the elements until you arrive at an educated guess. In general, but not always, a painting on canvas will fetch a larger price than a painting on paper. A one-of-a kind piece will sell for more than a multiple. With multiple images, such as photographs or prints, the smaller the edition, the larger the asking price for each piece. For three-dimensional work, expect bronze sculptures to sell for more than paper ones. In the photographic market, the more archival (or permanent) the materials, the more collectors will pay. Thus, Cibachrome prints fetch more than Ektacolor prints because the colors retain their brilliance longer; platinum prints fetch more than silver prints because platinum is so expensive to work with. A work of art that takes six months to complete will need to be priced higher than one taking six days. And across the board, in every art genre, the larger the piece, the higher the price tag.

Another way of putting this is that the price of an artwork is dependent upon the following:

- Rarity. One-of-a-kind pieces are worth more than multiples.
- Cost of materials. Gold-leaf paintings sell for more than watercolors.
- Permanence. Paintings on canvas are worth more than paintings on paper.
- Productivity. An artist who paints three paintings a year can ask more for them than an artist who paints thirty paintings a year, assuming the art is obviously more labor intensive.
- Size. Bigger is almost always more expensive.

Another important consideration is an artist's track record. If an artist is a recognized international figure, he or she can command a higher sum. For artists who haven't yet reached that stature there are signposts that can signal a rise in prices. Look for indications of media attention, sold-out shows, museum exhibitions, and works sold at auction.

Lay off the Muses—it's a very tough dollar.

S. J. PERELMAN

At the beginning of your career, you want to place your work inside the standard price range for the type and size of work that you make, and at the lower end of that price range. The advantages to this strategy are many. By pricing the work low, you will begin the process of getting the work moving. More people will buy it, which means more people will want to buy it, and you will start to develop a following. Pricing the work low creates room for the prices to increase, which makes you look successful and places your work in even higher demand. The last thing you want is to have to reduce your prices because they were too high for the market in the first place. At every point in an artist's career, he or she should appear to be a rising star, rather than a falling one.

One San Francisco art dealer described a scenario he told me happens all too often. A young artist, hanging his work in his first show (in a nonprofit art gallery or some other noncommercial space) will price the work to match the prices of artists who have a much longer track record. The work is really priced too high for his place in the market, but he sells a piece or two to friends and well-wishers. Then a gallery picks him up, and he learns he has to lower his prices in order to be affordable to its collectors. Now the artist has a dilemma. If he doesn't lower his prices, he won't be able to enter the larger marketplace, and if he does, he risks alienating his early supporters. This is yet another reason for starting out low.

But be careful not to price the work too low. If it is listed too far beneath the current market, it will be hard for collectors to take it seriously.

Matters are further complicated by the fact that the market values for art change in relation to the economy as a whole. Many wonderful artists whose images were selling successfully with megadigit price tags during the boom of the 1980s, can't find buyers with big-enough wallets in the more austere 1990s. In addition, every professional you talk to has a different opinion. To try to lessen the confusion, I asked the people who know, the dealers, for their input. What follows are their responses to an informal telephone survey in which the staff of a randomly selected group of commercial art galleries was asked how a serious artist at the beginning of his/her professional career should price the artwork. The dealers answered these questions with difficulty, since without seeing an actual piece of art it is impossible to calculate an accurate price. Still, some of them were generous enough to try. The survey was conducted in summer 1997. Use this survey as a starting point only, since this kind of information is very time sensitive. Even though prices may change, the relationships between pricing parameters should stay about the same. Notice the pricing differences between mediums in the survey, as well as regional differences.

Invoicing procedures. Once a work of art has been sold, update your inventory list with the date of the sale, the name of the gallery or art consultant who made the sale, and the name, address, and phone number of the collector who bought the work, and the purchase price. Sometimes the gallery will neglect to pass on this information to you, either because they don't think you care about knowing it or because they prefer to keep their collector list private. Don't let this information slip away. People who buy your art are your supporters in the most literal sense, and you have a right and a need to know who they are and how to reach them. When, in the years to come, the Whitney Museum wants to mount your retrospective, you need to be able to tell them who owns your early work. Or, on a less happy note,

Gallery	4' x 6' painting on canvas	30" x 40" work on paper	8" x 10" black & white photo	16" x 20" Cibachrome print	Suggestions by gallery personnel
Atrium Gallery, St. Louis	$1,500–$2,000	$1,000	$300	$300	Take pricing directions from your dealer. He or she knows the market.
Gallery Paule Anglim, San Francisco	$500–$1,000	$300–$800	N/A	N/A	You need to price low to promote the work, to start the momentum.
Roy Boyd Gallery, Chicago	$1,500–$3,000	$600–$2,000	$250–$400	$400	What harm is there if someone gets your first five paintings at a price you consider too cheap? They will follow your career fairly faithfully, and it doesn't hurt to have friends.
Robert Brown Gallery, Washington, D.C.	$1,200–$1,500	$800	$200	$350	If you are working with a dealer, trust their instincts. If not, call up someone with more experience, and ask him or her to come over and give advice.
D.O.C.S. Gallery, New Orleans	$1,500	$700–$1,000	$250	$350	Price the work to sell.
Kim Foster Gallery, NYC	$2,000–$3,000	$1,200	$300	$400	Artists should get to know a gallery first, before they approach them.
Sherry Frumkin Gallery, Santa Monica	$3,000–$6,000	$800–$1,500	$500–$800	$900–$1,500	Galleries will price work differently based on their clientele.
G. Gibson Gallery, Seattle	N/A	N/A	$50–$300	$250–$500	These prices are for artists without gallery representation.
Allene LaPides Gallery, Santa Fe	$1,000–$1,400	$500–$700	$50–$80	N/A	Be modest in your pricing. You can always go up, but you can't go down. Find a dealer you can trust, not just someone who wants you.
Mangel Gallery, Philadelphia	$400–$3,000	$300–$750	N/A	N/A	If the artist is brand new and doesn't have any benchmarks, it is difficult to determine prices. The price will depend upon how good the artist is.
Vance Martin, San Francisco	N/A	$750	$300–$400	$550–$600	These prices are for work shown in a gallery; if shown elsewhere the prices should be lower.
MC Gallery, Minneapolis	$1,200–$1,500	$800	$350	$400	The value of the work is based on supply and demand; at the beginning of your career there is no demand, so price the work as low as you can live with.
Yancey Richardson Gallery, NYC	N/A	N/A	$300–$400	$500	The more professional artists become, the better for those of us who are dealers.
SFMOMA Rental Gallery, San Francisco	$1,200–$2,000	$650 framed	$200–$400	N/A	These prices may seem low, but you need to remember that prices became inflated in the 1980s and have now fallen.
Zolla/Lieberman Gallery, Chicago	$1,500–$2,000	$800	N/A	N/A	Don't be afraid to price low. It's better to have your work in a collector's home than in your studio.

A Simple Invoice (printed on your letterhead)

Date: Invoice number (optional):
Sold to: Name
            Address

Title of piece: *Retail price:*

"Unique Masterpiece" $1,000.00
Edition # 499/500
1998
gelatin silver print

Dealer discount 50%   −500.00

Subtotal $500.00

Tax (if applicable, added when selling directly to the client)   0.00

TOTAL DUE $500.00

Work shipped to above address by UPS on Tuesday, April 10, 1998.

Payment due upon receipt of invoice.

---

if you and your gallery have a falling out, you don't want to lose your collectors as well.

Write an invoice for every sale, regardless of who sold it or where, and even if you have already been paid. Give a copy to the client, and put another in your files. You can design an invoice form specifically for the purpose, or just use your letterhead. The invoice information should include the date; the name of the gallery, if applicable; title, date, and description of the purchase; retail price and any commissions or discounts you have agreed to; and the total due and amount received. If the work was sold from the gallery's inventory, indicate it on the invoice. If it was shipped from your studio, note the method of shipping. An up-to-date invoice system is an excellent way of keeping track of the state of your business. It provides easy access to information when doing your taxes, and, if necessary, will serve as proof to the IRS that you are indeed a working artist.

Shipping Your Art

In preparing art for shipping, anticipate what could go wrong and plan for it. The packaging should be made of strong water-repellent materials that absorb shock and are easily handled. If the packing materials are to be used for return shipping, they should come apart and go together again without self-destructing or creating extra work for the person receiving the package. Depending on the type of art to be shipped, materials to keep on hand for shipping might include corrugated cardboard, $1/8$-inch masonite, plywood crates, bubble wrap or Styrofoam popcorn, plastic sheeting or bags to wrap the art in, plastic shipping tape, and strapping tape.

Always do right. This will gratify some people and astonish the rest.

MARK TWAIN

A simple and effective method for shipping two-dimensional objects such as unframed drawings or prints is to place the art between two slightly larger pieces of masonite and cover the masonite with a layer of cardboard on each side. The masonite is strong enough to protect the work from almost any kind of shipping damage, and the slightly larger size will protect the corners of the artwork, the most vulnerable part. This larger size package will also protect the work of art from knife damage when it is opened. The cardboard adds an extra layer of strength.

The procedure is as follows:
- Place the artwork inside a plastic bag (an archival brand if possible), and cut a small hole in the bag to allow excess air to escape.
- Place the plastic bag in the center of a piece of masonite. Two inches of masonite should be visible around each edge of the artwork.

- Tape the work at all four corners so it doesn't slip.
- Place the consignment forms to be signed by the recipient on top of the art, taking care that there are no staples, paper clips, or rough surfaces which could damage the art.
- Place the second piece of masonite on top of the first, creating a sandwich.
- Put a piece of tape on each side of the sandwich to hold it together.
- Insert the sandwich between two pieces of corrugated cardboard (with the ridges of each piece going in opposite directions to increase strength).
- Cover all four sides with plastic shipping tape.
- The package is ready to be addressed.

Framed pieces and three-dimensional art work will need to be shipped in a crate, which should be slightly larger than the art. The area around the art should be filled with materials that protect and cushion the work and firmly hold it in place. Most shipping crates are constructed of plywood with screws rather than nails so that they can be opened quickly and reused easily. Never send glass through the mail. If you are shipping framed pieces, be careful to use Plexiglas instead of glass.

For detailed information about preparing different kinds of art for shipping I suggest the clear and concise *Way To Go*, written by Stephen Horne and published by the Gallery Association of New York State. Shipping materials such as cardboard and Plexiglas can be found at any art supply store as well as some packaging and plastic supply stores, masonite and plywood at your local lumber yard, and bubble wrap and custom-made cardboard boxes at a mailing supply store. For ready-made shipping cases designed specifically for shipping art, see the appendix in this book, or look for advertisements in art magazines.

Shipping companies. The safest and most professional way to ship art is to hire an art shipping company to do it for you. Unfortunately this is also the most expensive, often prohibitively so for many artists. Most galleries don't use them either, unless the art is particularly difficult to handle; they prefer to use less-expensive carriers. The most

There is a thin line between genius and insanity. I have erased this line.
OSCAR LEVANT

CARDBOARD

MASONITE

CONSIGNMENT
FORM

Consignment Form

ART IN
PLASTIC BAG

MASONITE

CARDBOARD

SHIPPING FLAT ART

affordable, UPS, can be quite safe, providing you take some precautions. The first is to package the work well, protecting it with a strong layer of wood (such as the masonite suggested above). The second is to purchase extra insurance up to the full value of the work. Shipping insurance is inexpensive and can really help soothe your broken heart if something should go wrong with the package en route to its destination. Federal Express and other carriers are also good choices for shipping your work. They all, including UPS, have size limitations, so check with them first about current regulations.

My own experience with UPS has primarily been a happy one. It has shipped my work for many years, with only one problem delivery. An art gallery in Los Angeles had shown my slides to a collector, who promptly bought four pieces and requested that I ship them from inventory. I packaged the prints as I suggested above, with two pieces of masonite inside a cardboard cover, but when the package arrived, it had been folded in half. The masonite was broken, and the artwork mutilated. I still haven't figured out how that happened. The gallery owner pulled out her trusty Polaroid camera and took pictures of the package before she opened it, then called UPS to report it. The UPS office sent an inspector, who agreed that the shipping company was definitely at fault. Since I had purchased insurance from UPS to the full value of the work, they had no choice but to pay up. I got busy printing another set of photographs for the client. In the meantime, another collector came into the gallery, saw the damaged photographs, and decided he wanted a set for himself. I was ultimately paid for twelve photographs instead of four. Not a bad day's work, but it could have been an unhappy one if I had cut corners on packaging or insurance.

Too much complaining and too little work.

GEORGIA O'KEEFFE

� Developing and Maintaining a Mailing List

As an artist, one of the most powerful things you can do for your career is to create, maintain, and *use* an up-to-date mailing list. Making a habit of sending announcements to the people on your list whenever you have an exhibition will go a long way toward advancing your career. The perfect mailing list contains the names and addresses of all your past and present supporters, as well as of people you hope will support you in the future. Keep this list on a computer disk, so that it will be easy to add and delete names and make address changes. Start your list with your current address book and include everyone you know and interact with in your daily life. Include friends and family, of course, but don't forget your coworkers, doctor, dentist, and insurance man. These people may be among your first collectors.

After these people, add the names and addresses of the art professionals in your geographic area. You can locate this information in local newspapers, regional art periodicals, and your August issue of *Art in America*. Be sure to include the name of the appropriate contact person for the type of art that you make. If there is an art museum in your city, telephone and ask the name and job title of the painting curator (or photography curator, etc.), so that your mailing list is exactly tailored to the people you want to reach. It should include curators at museums and nonprofit spaces, gallery directors, and art critics.

Eventually you will want to compile a list of the top national and international art professionals in your area of interest. As part of your campaign to generate interest in your work, make a habit of mailing an announcement to each of them at every opportunity, particularly if the announcement carries a picture of your work. Curators in Chicago may not travel to Texas to see an exhibition, but receiving the announcement will begin the process of making them aware of who you are.

Maintaining a mailing list can be an endless chore. People are constantly moving and changing jobs, and there are always new people to add and others to delete. Almost by definition, your mailing list will be out of date. Update information regularly, weekly if you can, so that the job doesn't become too daunting. There are many mailing list computer programs on the market. I use BulkMailer, but a list can be created and maintained in Now Contact, ClarisWorks, Filemaker, and many more.

I love deadlines. I like the whooshing sound they make as they fly by.
DOUGLAS ADAMS

Preparing for the Tax Man

Doing your taxes as an artist is not much more difficult than what you are doing already. You will need to add a Schedule C (Profit or Loss from Business or Profession) to your tax return, keep clear records, and save receipts and show announcements. None of this is difficult, but it should be done fastidiously in case you ever have to explain yourself to the Internal Revenue Service.

The IRS has never taken very kindly to artists. This is because no self-respecting IRS man can believe that anyone would willingly participate in an activity that doesn't turn a profit. Being the distrustful people that they are, IRS inspectors assume that being a starving artist must be some fancy tax dodge. Their job, as they see it, is to prove that you are an amateur so that your expenses won't be deductible. The best way to thwart them is to make money. The second best way is to *try* to make money.

The IRS looks for certain signals that you are indeed a professional artist. Jo Hanson, an artist who has been audited by the IRS eight times, and has beaten them at their own game every time, has written a marvelous (and short) book called *Artists' Taxes: The Hands-on*

Guide, in which she lists the activities the IRS examines. According to Hanson, you should keep a record of sales and customers (your invoices will suffice), maintain an inventory of work for sale (your inventory list), keep receipt and expense records (save all business receipts), and keep a separate bank account for your art activities. If you don't want to incur the expense of a separate bank account, you can use your personal account as long as you make a note next to each check designating whether it was written for business or personal use.

If the IRS wants proof that you are a professional artist, give it to them. You are already doing all these things anyway, just make sure your records are complete.

- Maintain a mailing list, which is proof of your connection to your clients.
- Send out announcements of all your art activities (proof of attempts to attract more clients).
- Save at least one announcement from each show (proof that the show actually did happen).
- Keep copies of all your cover letters to galleries (proof that you are trying to sell).
- File copies of the letters you receive in return (proof that others are responding).

All of these activities are indications that you are behaving as any business person would to try to grow your business. Taking these measures will lift you out of the realm of "hobbyist" and force the IRS to take you seriously.

I hope you will never have to discuss these things with the IRS. If all the lines on your tax form are properly filled out and free from mathematical errors, and if there are no outrageously large or unusual deductions, you should be okay. If you can afford it, have an accountant do your taxes. Then, if you do get audited, you will have a professional to help you deal with it.

The saints are the sinners who keep on going.

ROBERT LOUIS
STEVENSON

CHAPTER SEVEN

Staging an Art Exhibition

Conceiving and producing your own exhibition, rather than sitting and waiting for the art world to take notice of you, can be an exhilarating way to enter public life as an artist. In the process you will learn how to plan, mount, and publicize a show and develop an understanding of the amount of work involved and what needs to be attended to when. These skills can free you from the tyranny of the gallery system; or, if you decide to work with a gallery, they will place you in a better position to know when your dealers are doing their job. A successful exhibition can bring art to a larger audience, improve the neighborhood, and provide quite an adrenaline rush for you.

You will need to decide whether to put on a solo exhibition or to include other artists. A one-person show looks better on the resume, but a group show usually attracts more people. With a group or two-person show, the work can be shared among the participants so that no one person has to do it all. Attendance will be multiplied since each artist will be inviting people from his or her own support group, costs can be shared, and you will have someone to laugh and cry with. If you mount a solo show you will gain all the glory, and you won't have to deal with possible personality conflicts, which can sometimes emerge when any group of people tries to work together. Regardless of the style of exhibition you decide upon, planning ahead will be the key to your success.

Finding a space to hold the show. Any building with empty walls is a good candidate to house your exhibition. Start by checking out public spaces like cafés and government buildings that already have exhibition programs in place, but don't limit yourself to those possibilities. Go on a reconnaissance mission to the area of town where you would like to hold your show. Look for hallways in corporate buildings, large meeting rooms, library spaces, church meeting areas, empty storefronts, companies and organizations with lovely, pristine spaces just waiting for your art to grace them. If you choose a location not ordinarily used for art exhibitions, you may be able to take advantage of the uniqueness of the event when writing publicity for the show.

When approaching the owner of the space, be friendly and businesslike. The idea is to convince them that you will act responsibly when using their building and that you will be open and reasonable in your dealings with them. Bring slides of at least some of the artwork to be shown, so that they will have a visual cue on which to base a decision, particularly if the art is difficult work. You don't want to have to cope with censorship issues later on. If you are dealing with a large organization, try to avoid discussing your proposal with people at the

There is nothing new in art except talent.
ANTON CHEKHOV

Exhibition Time Line

At least three months before the show:
Find exhibition space.
Decide on show dates.
Decide on reception date.
Decide on show title.
Delegate tasks.
Photograph sample artwork for black
    and white glossies for press release.
Telephone local newspapers and
    magazines to find out press release
    lead times.

Ten weeks before the show:
Write the press release.

Eight weeks before the show:
Mail press release. (May need to be
    mailed slightly earlier or later
    depending on the publication.)
Design announcement.

Six weeks before the show:
Take announcement to printer.
Update mailing list.

One month before the show:
Make final decisions about which
    art to include.
Frame the art.
Buy stamps, labels, and other supplies for
    mailing announcements.
Assemble binder with bio, statement,
    and slides for each artist in the
    show.

Two weeks before the show:
Mail announcements.
Plan and order food for the reception.
Decide what you are going to wear.
Line up helpers to take care of food
    and sales at the reception.
Make a description label for each piece
    in the show.
Write price list.

Several days before the show:
Hang work.
Round up nonperishable reception supplies
    and a reception book for visitors to sign.
Make last-minute changes in labels and price
    list.

Before the reception:
Purchase perishable foods.
Set up refreshment table.
Set up guest book, slide binder, and slide
    viewer (optional).

At the reception:
Make visitors feel welcome.
Have fun.

During the run of the exhibition:
Arrange private tours.

After the show:
Take down the art.
Deliver pieces to people who bought them.
Repair and paint gallery walls.

middle-management level. They are usually in no position to make a decision and tend to slow down the process. Ask to speak to the owner, and when you reach him or her, don't spare the flattery. People who have built their own businesses are usually proud of them. You can gain a lot by letting them know how much you would like your art to be shown in their environment.

Most of the time you will find that people are thrilled at the prospect of hosting an art show. Occasionally you will encounter someone who is reluctant for insurance or other reasons. Unless you really must have that space, let it go and move on to your second choice. You will find lots of people who are delighted to hang your art. If the building you have chosen is empty, the building owner may ask for some sort of rent payment in exchange for use of the premises. You may be able to bring this cost down, particularly if the building has gone unused for a long time, by explaining that you only need the space for a short time (one to three months), that your very presence will improve the property (by cleaning, painting, if necessary), and that the publicity involved with the exhibition will bring attention to the building itself, thus showing it off to advantage to any prospective tenants.

If you are looking for a space not usually used for exhibitions, be sure to consider, and discuss with the owner, how the work will be mounted on the wall. You don't want to find out later that the wallpaper is covering concrete, or that the owner refuses to allow you to put any holes in the walls; this makes it very difficult to hang art.

Deciding on exhibition dates. The traditional time period for an art exhibition is one month, but for your purposes six weeks is better. You want to allow plenty of time for the publicity to take effect. In order for most weekly and biweekly publications to consider reviewing a show, the art should be on view for at least four weeks. If the reviewer sees the show in the first week and writes the article the next week, and the publication prints it the third week, that leaves very little time for people reading the review to get down to the gallery. Most magazines require that the show be hung for even longer, since they only publish once a month.

Some of the world's greatest feats were accomplished by people not smart enough to know they were impossible.

DOUG LARSON

Group Show Tasks

Show Coordinator: This person acts as the gallery liaison, ascertaining things like the amount of wall space available, how much time will be allotted to hanging the show, the quality of the lighting, and special requests or expectations of the building owner. This person will also be the committee coordinator and the central clearing house for information among the artists in the show. This is not a job for a general; find someone less bossy, more like a diplomat, otherwise everyone will become irritated.

Installation Chairperson: Oversees the installation and removal of the exhibition. If necessary, returns the walls to their previous condition. Ideally, the Installation Chair should have a committee of three to five people, depending on the size of the show and the amount of time scheduled for installing it. He or she should know how to use a hammer and a level.

Written Materials Coordinator: Completes the finishing touches for the show, including designing and printing the labels to be installed next to the art, preparing the price list, purchasing the guest book, and organizing a three-ring binder with bios, statements, and slides of all the artists in the show. This is a good job for someone with computer skills.

Reception Coordinator: Coordinates the food and wine for the reception, and the clean-up after it. Recruits several nonartist helpers to attend to the food table and the bar during the reception.

Announcement Designer: Designs the announcement for the show, oversees the printing, buys the stamps, prints the mailing labels, and coordinates the mailing party. Graphic design experience is helpful, but not necessary.

Press Release Committee: Writes the press release, copies it, collects black and white glossy photos from the artists, puts together press packets, and mails them. The ideal committee should consist of several people, so that no one has to assemble the mailing alone.

The reception can be held at the beginning (an opening reception) or the end of the show (a closing reception). An opening reception is preferable because it gives the viewers time to return a second and third time, perhaps to view a piece they were taken with or to bring friends. Schedule the opening reception a few days after you actually hang the show, so there is time to remedy any unforeseen problems and get some rest before the event.

Deciding on the show title. The show may or may not have a title or theme. If it is a one-person show, the title can be something like *Betty Boop: Recent Work* or, if the art in the show is from a specific series, *Betty Boop: Lipstick Paintings.* The more specific (and interesting) the title is, the more people it is likely to bring in. If you wish to attract the attention of the press, you will want to have a catchy title.

Finding a title for a group show can sometimes be a challenge, depending on how much the artists have in common. If possible, chose artists whose work has some relationship to yours so that a theme becomes obvious. If there is no apparent theme uniting the work, get together and brainstorm. You'll be surprised at the wonderful and/or outrageous ideas a group of creative people can come up with. If you find you can't agree on anything, a simple listing of the artists names will be fine.

Delegating Tasks

Whether yours is to be a one-person show or will include a cast of thousands, planning ahead for the various tasks is essential. If the show is all yours, you will need to ask friends for help, enlist the aid of your studio assistant, or hire outside help for at least part of the work. The following is a task breakdown for a group show. For a solo exhibition, go over the checklist with an eye toward planning when and where you will ask for assistance. If necessary, you can do almost all the tasks by yourself, but they will take longer to complete.

Making black and white glossies for the press release. An editor is more likely to notice a press release if it is accompanied by a photograph, and if it is noticed, the show is more likely to be reviewed and the photo reproduced. The press print should be a black and white glossy photograph, printed in either an 8" x 10" or 5" x 7" format. I suggest 5" x 7" because it costs less and the quality doesn't seem to suffer in reproduction.

In deciding which piece of art to use for the press release, look for a catchy and easily readable image. It should translate well to black and white. If you choose a simpler and more graphic image—one with less subtlety and complexity—it will look better when reproduced in a publication. Try standing in front of your paintings and squinting at them to approximate the effect of a black and white rendition. Notice that some areas of the painting that may in reality look quite lovely start to look muddy or lost when you squint. Choose artwork that looks crisp and clear. You only need one piece.

Once you have decided upon the piece (or pieces) for the press print, photograph it with black and white film. Print enough copies of the image to include one in each press packet you intend to mail. Photographic labs charge by quantity, so the more you print from the same negative, the less you will pay per print. If you print, say, fifty copies of one image, your cost will be much less than for one copy of fifty images.

With an apple, I will astonish Paris.

PAUL CEZANNE

Writing the press release. The press release should be written following a standard form that should not be deviated from. Publications receive thousands of press releases, and the person in charge of receiving and reading them will usually not be amenable to giving extra time to anything that makes his or her job more difficult. The purpose of the press release is to entice the publication to write about the show, doing so in the simplest, most direct manner possible.

The press release should be printed on official-looking letterhead. You may use your personal stationery, or a letterhead designed to reflect the group. Begin with the words "Press Release" at the top and in the center. Underneath, on the left-hand side, the word "Contact," followed by a name and phone number, should be prominently displayed. Opposite the contact name and on the same line, type the words "For Immediate Release." If the event will include some unusual or visually interesting activity, or the presence of a controversial or famous person, add the words "Photo Opportunity."

— *P R E S S   R E L E A S E* —

CONTACT: Jane of the Jungle

(212) 555-1111

FOR IMMEDIATE RELEASE

(Photo Opportunity)

PHOTOGRAPHS BY TROUBLED CHIMPANZEES

— WORLD PREMIERE —

January 31, 1998

For the first time in human history, the African Chimpanzee community will exhibit recent photographs by prominent artists in a two-month exhibition at the See-No-Evil Gallery, 123 West 57th Street, New York, NY. The exhibition will open on April 1, 1998, and run through May 30. The opening reception is Friday, April 3, from 5:00 to 7:00 P.M. Works included in the exhibition are 20" x 24" Ektacolor prints from the Old Leaf Series by Wally Cole, 30" x 40" silver prints from the Troubled Water Series by Brenda Whitney, and 16" x 20" Cibachromes from the Friendly Lice Series by Sam de Vader.

Well-known in their native habitat, artists in this exhibition present their work for the first time to the human community. The works deal with issues of alienation, ecology, and species prejudice.

Wally Cole, who recently changed his name from Abdul the Great, presents twenty Ektacolor prints that examine the evolution of leaves produced by the trees in his backyard in Kenya. The photographs, taken over a fifteen-year period, poignantly reveal the heroic struggle for survival these trees endure.

Brenda Whitney, a recent émigré from the Congo, creates her work by immersing black and white film in samples of water from the Congo River. The result is a series of eerily corroded negatives that are then placed in an enlarger and printed to 30" x 40". Hauntingly beautiful, yet emotionally disturbing, these images make visible unseen terrors hiding in the water.

Sam de Vader has spent the last five years learning to speak the language of lice. Communicating by elaborate hand and leg gestures, along with a series of small bites (or "nips" as they call them), African lice have developed a sophisticated language. De Vader's photographs create a glimpse into the intricacies of this language.

###

The press release should have a headline. This is meant to be an attention-grabber, so try to make it as interesting as possible.

The most important information (who, what, where, when, how, and maybe why) should be written concisely into the first paragraph. A busy editor may only read this far before making up his or her mind, so write the first paragraph as though it is the only chance you have to get his attention. Editors tend to look for press releases they can steal sentences from; it makes their job so much easier. Write yours with their interests in mind.

The rest of the press release can elaborate on the information presented in the first paragraph, with each successive paragraph being less important than the one before it. Aim for brevity. Don't exceed two pages for the entire document; one is even better. Finish the document by typing three number signs in a row (###). This convention indicates the end of the press release.

Mailing the press release. If you are enclosing a black and white glossy photograph with your press release, you will need to mail it in a manila envelope large enough to contain the press release, the glossy, a piece of thin cardboard for stiffness, and a return SASE (if you hope to have your materials returned). If you are mailing the press release by itself, an ordinary business envelope will do.

Putting together a press-release mailing list is an ongoing project. Like your other mailing lists, expect it to be constantly changing. Ideally, the list should include everyone in a position to publicize your art. Start locally. Telephone the newspapers, magazines, art journals, and television and radio stations. Ask them for the names of arts writers, feature writers, editors, and the person in charge of the calendar listings. Add each name to your press-release list and address them in care of the publication they work for, unless they request otherwise.

The press release should be mailed no later than eight weeks before the opening of the show in order to allow time for the writers to respond. Once you have created your list, print the labels, buy supplies—stamps, envelopes, cardboard, and beer—and hold a mailing party. Place a good-luck kiss on each packet before dropping it in the mailbox.

Life is a great big canvas, and you should throw all the paint on it you can.

DANNY KAYE

Designing the announcement. The primary purpose of the show announcement is to generate attendance at the show. It should indicate where the show is being held, the theme or title of the show, the dates of the exhibition, the reception date and time, and the gallery hours. If the flyer announces a group show, the names of all the artists in the exhibition should be prominent; don't just print the title of the show alone. Part of the purpose of the announcement is to create name recognition for the artists involved, and that's difficult if their names are not included.

In designing an announcement for a one-person show, seriously consider including a color reproduction of one of your pieces. Look for a printing company that specializes in printing full-color exhibition invitations at reasonable prices. I have listed a few in the appendix. Others are often listed in the advertising section of local and national art magazines. Look for companies that print full-color postcards or greeting cards in relatively short runs. A color announcement with a picture will cost more than other announcements, but the advantages are many. Seeing an image of one of the artworks before the show can often convince an undecided collector to attend the event. An announcement with an image on it can provide a glimpse of the show for those people who live too far away to travel to the exhibition. Sometimes the picture alone can create a sale. I once received a phone call from a collector in Texas I had never met. She had seen the full-color announcement I had sent to a colleague and called to buy the piece over the phone.

An announcement with an image on it will continue to work for you after the show is over. Include it in your promotional packet along with your slides, bio, and statement to add another layer of credibility to your career. If you can afford it, print extra announcements just for this purpose.

Early in my career, I sent a full-color reproduction of one of my photographs to a curator at the Palais de Tokyo in Paris. Although the show was in California and I had never met the curator, I had always hoped I would someday take my work to Paris. A year later I was able to go, and when I arrived I discovered my announcement pinned to the bulletin board next to her desk. I was thrilled! She had liked the image enough to hang it where she could see it every day. Not only

> And the trouble is,
> if you don't risk
> anything, you risk
> even more.
>
> ERICA JONG

did she see it every day, but everyone who walked through her office saw it as well. You can't get better advertising than that.

Costs for printing an announcement can vary widely. The cheapest way to print an announcement is to copy it onto card stock at your local copy center. You will be limited to black ink, but you can use colored stock; and if the card is well-designed, it can look quite nice. Avoid large areas of black when designing the card, since copy machines often have uneven ink coverage.

The next step up in quality and cost is a one-color print. Black ink is the cheapest, but switching to another color doesn't add much to the cost and can make a striking card. Most show announcements are one-color prints, and, if well-designed, they can look very enticing. This is a good choice for a group show announcement if cost is an issue.

Success is a matter of luck—ask any failure.

EARL WILSON

A two-color print can look as sophisticated as full-color at about half the cost. Two colors can also combine to create the illusion of a third color.

A three-color print is almost never done because it costs as much as a full-color print to produce. Full-color printing can be very expensive, unless you use one of the companies that specialize in "ganging" (or grouping) announcements to cut production costs. These companies combine many artists' postcards on the same sheet of paper when printing, thereby reducing the costs for the individual artists. The disadvantage to gang printing is that the printer can't always match colors exactly in all the cards, since so many different kinds of images will be printed together. If you are lucky, the press operator will concentrate on matching yours. If you choose a local company to print your announcement, ask to be present at the press run so you will be in a position to suggest changes, if necessary.

Other factors can add to the printing costs of your announcement. Using a photograph will increase the cost, as will "bleeding" an image or a block of color. A bleed is when the ink runs off the edges of the paper. This apparently creates extra work for the printer, so he or she will add an extra fee to your bill. Printing on both sides of the paper increases the cost as well, as does the choice of an expensive paper. If the paper is "coated" or very thick, it will cost more. The surface of coated paper is specially treated to make it take ink crisply and smoothly. If you are reproducing an image, you will want to use coated stock.

Size is also a factor to be considered. The smaller the announcement, the more you can print on one sheet of paper; the less paper you use, the more money you save. A small announcement will save postage costs as well. Check with the post office for the current regulations. If the announcement is small enough it can be sent at postcard rates, otherwise it will be sent at the letter rate. The post office also has rules about oversize letters. If the card measures over a certain size, the post office will charge you extra.

Regardless of the type of card you print, proofread it carefully. You'll be surprised how often errors are overlooked. Especially check the numbers—dates, times, and street addresses—since numbers frequently look right even if they are incorrect. You don't want people showing up for the reception on the wrong day.

I always keep my eyes open for great show announcements and flyers printed in interesting ways. When I find one, I throw it in a file so that when it's time to design my next announcement, I have plenty of good examples to start with.

Working with a printer. Once you have a rough idea of the layout of your announcement, show it to your printer. He or she may have some suggestions for improving it, but most importantly the printer will know if the shop's equipment can handle the job that you intend to print. Sometimes just changing the size of the card by a fraction of an inch can save a substantial amount of money and time. Your printer can show you paper and ink samples and explain the cost variables. Ask to see examples of previous printing jobs. If the quality isn't up to your standards look for another printer. Find out how long it will take to complete the job. It's a good idea to agree on a timeline in advance so the announcements will be certain to be ready. Get the work to the printer early so if anything goes wrong, there is time to correct it.

Mailing the announcement. The main purpose of the announcement is to entice people to attend the reception, and, if not the reception, then to visit the exhibition during its run. Mail the announcement two weeks prior to the opening of the show so that, when it arrives, the receiver will have enough time to plan ahead for the event, but not so much time that he or she forgets about it. Hand-write a short note on cards to people you know, or want to know, as an added inducement to attend. It doesn't matter what you say; the fact that you took the time to write a personal message will have a positive effect. "Looking forward to seeing you" and "Come celebrate with me," or even "Hi, Betty!" are appropriate notes. Don't pretend you know the person if you really don't under the misguided assumption that they will think they must have met you somewhere and so feel compelled to come. Your ploy will be obvious, and it will only serve to convince them never to come near you. If your work appears in a show with several artists, highlight your name with a felt pen when sending the announcement to your personal mailing list.

Imagination is more important than knowledge.

ALBERT EINSTEIN

I always love holding a mailing party when I have a lot of invitations to send out. You will need some willing friends, the invitations, a mailing list printed on labels, stamps, sponges, refreshments, and an evening to spare.

You will probably be using first class stamps for your mailing unless you want to send it bulk mail, which demands a lot of extra time and work for very little savings in cost. Consider getting a bulk-rate permit only if you are sending an extremely large mailing, particularly if you intend to do it more than once a year. Be prepared to pay a yearly fee to the post office for the permit, and an extra fee if you want the number preprinted on the card (thus avoiding hours of stamp-licking). You will also be expected to presort the mail according to post office regulations (which are elaborate, but not difficult). If you don't have the time or the energy to prepare the mailing yourself, there are companies who will do it for you. Prices and services vary, so call several before you make up your mind. You can find them in the yellow pages under mailing services.

Framing the art. A whole book can be written about framing, and several have been (and are listed in the appendix). I am going to assume, just for the moment anyway, that you are not interested in becoming a professional framer, and will concentrate instead on current practices and prejudices in framing contemporary art. Framing styles go in and out of fashion, just as art does, so you will need to know the doctrine of the day in order to make conscious choices concerning it.

The main rule of thumb when framing contemporary art is that no part of the framing structure (this includes the mattes) should take the viewer's attention away from the art, unless the frame itself is part of the piece. Translate this to mean: choose a simple frame, one without curlicues, gold accents, or a fabric inlay. If you are matting the art, the matte should be made of 100 percent rag (for archival protection of the art) and should always be white, off-white, or occasionally black or gray. Never ever use a colored matte, especially not one with layered colors surrounding the image, even if your framer suggests it. Colored mattes are red flags to today's curators and critics. They scream "Amateur." Framers like to suggest layered and colored mattes because it's more interesting for them to create a complicated frame, and they can charge more for it. You don't want an interesting frame. You want a frame that makes the art stand out.

If the work is very postmodern, you may decide to add an elaborate frame as a tongue-in-cheek comment on the culture. Artists who work in this mode think of the frame as a part of the art and make their choices based on this.

If you visit a top commercial gallery, you will see several variations on framing. Small to medium-size pieces will be framed in simple wood or metal frames with white mattes. Large paintings will either be painted around the edges of the stretcher bars or enclosed in thin strips of wood or metal. Occasionally you will see strange clunky-looking frames with stuff glued to them or sleek wide frames made out of sheets of metal, or boxes made out of Plexiglas, but in each case, to prevent the presentation from looking amateurish, the reason for an unusual framing decision should be obvious.

As for expenses, the more you do yourself, the less the frames will cost you. The cheapest and most versatile framing method is to purchase metal frames from a mail-order company and assemble them with a screwdriver. You will also need Plexiglas, a backing board (a piece of cardboard the same size as the Plexiglas), and wire or brackets for hanging the work. If the work is to be matted, you can buy a matte-cutter and archival board and cut them yourself (be prepared to make lots of mistakes at first), or shop them out to a framer. A framer mattes work every day, so if you want perfect mattes and don't have time to develop the skill, this might be a good choice for you.

If you can afford it, consider having a framer do it all, particularly if you are interested in a wooden frame, since these take a little more skill to assemble. To find a good framer, call a local gallery whose art looks well-framed and ask who they use. Galleries always know the name of the least expensive good framer in town.

Hanging the show. General decisions on what will be included in the show should be made long before the actual installation begins. With a group show, since everyone's work will be a different size, a fair way to divide the exhibition area is to measure the total wall space in the gallery and divide it by the number of artists in the show. A hundred feet of wall space divided by ten artists will result in an allotment of

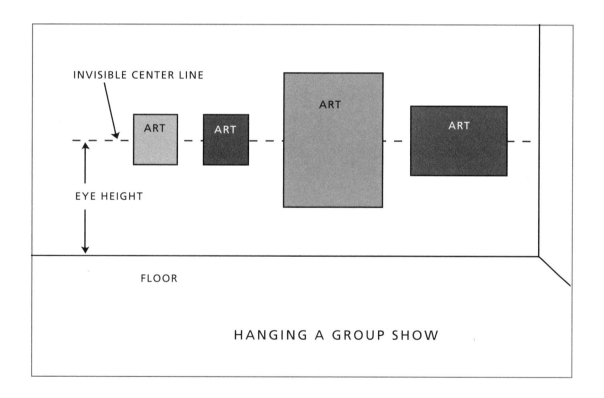

ten feet each. It is up to each artist to decide how to use his allotted space. If an artist makes eight-foot paintings, he or she will only be able to hang one piece in the show; if the work is the size of a postcard, many more can be exhibited in the space. If an artist makes sculpture or installation art, adjustments may need to be made in the allotment of space

On the day of the installation, all the art should arrive at the exhibition site ready to hang. That means the framing decisions have already been made and carried out and the pieces are finished right down to the wires on the back. Start by placing each piece on the floor in front of a section of the wall you think will compliment it. Do not hang anything until all the pieces are placed. This is particularly important with a group show since, by definition, it is a group effort and each participant needs to be satisfied with the result.

A few rules of thumb for placing the work: Start with the problem pieces first, the ones that can only hang in a few locations either because they are very large, very fragile, or employ sculptural elements. Once you have these placed, a pattern will begin to suggest itself, and the other art will find its spot. Try to keep all the work by one artist in the same location, creating a series of mini solo shows within the larger show. Sculpture presents a special problem. It will need to occupy floor space in a location where it cannot be easily damaged or stolen, and will not cause an accident.

Theft is not often a problem in an art show, but it does happen; and a few precautions can be taken to save your work from light-fingered art lovers. If the art is a wall-piece such as a painting or drawing, there are special security hanging devices available that attach the art securely to the wall. The Oz Clip is the most common. For small sculpture on a pedestal, construct a Plexiglas box to fit on top of the pedestal and attach it to the pedestal with screws. A thief will have to carry off the entire pedestal in order to steal the sculpture.

You will need supplies and a set of tools for installing the show. Bring lots of nails and picture hangers, a hammer for pounding them, a tape measure, a level for checking the straightness of your work, and cotton gloves to protect both the art and your hands. Bring pliers or wire cutters in case you need to adjust the wire on the back of some of the pieces, and extra wire in case you screw up. You will need glass and Plexiglas cleaner for removing fingerprints, as well as soft cloths and paper towels. You also may need to bring a ladder.

Hang the show so that the center point of each piece is at eye level. Stand back from the work and imagine an invisible line going through the middle of each piece and parallel to the floor. Or don't imagine it. Make it easy and get a string and stretch it temporarily across the wall, securing it with a couple of push pins. Adjust the art up or down in relation to this line. Now check to see if there is enough room between each piece. You should be able to look at each work of art without having the piece next to it insist on equal time. It is okay to glimpse other pieces with your peripheral vision, but it should be clear that each piece in the show is meant to be enjoyed as its own experience. If two paintings are placed too close together, they will be seen as one piece. Hanging too many pieces in a show is a common mistake of amateur artists, so a good rule of thumb is: Once you have placed the work, remove one piece from each wall.

When attaching a piece on the wall, use two nails rather than one so that it will remain level. Once the piece is up, place a level on top to check that it is straight, tugging it slightly one way or the other until you are satisfied with the result.

When all the artwork is hung, next adjust the lighting. If you are lucky enough to be using a gallery blessed with track lighting, this is a simple matter. Climb up a ladder and aim the lights at the art. The lighting should be even across the entire piece, and it may take several lights to accomplish this if the artwork is large. You can also change the light bulbs from spotlights to floodlights or vice versa. Spots provide a beam of concentrated light in one area, while floodlights spread the light over a wider surface.

If the show is hung in a hallway or a public building, examine the existing lighting. Often the simple act of changing a light bulb can make a dramatic difference. The worst situation is a room full of fluorescent lights. Standard fluorescent lights have a greenish tinge that can make almost any art piece look washed out. The good news is that daylight-balanced fluorescent bulbs are available. If the space comes equipped with regular tungsten lights (normal light bulbs), switch to quartz lights. You can learn about lighting options from a store that specializes in light bulbs, or go to a place like Home Depot and talk to the resident expert. If you will be buying quite a few bulbs, you can sometimes convince the shop proprietor to lend you several to try out first.

If all else fails, there are always clip-on lights. Almost every hardware store sells them. Look for the kind with a ceramic base rather than a plastic one. The plastic can melt when using high-voltage light bulbs, creating a fire hazard.

Descriptive labels should be hung on the wall next to each art piece, always on the same side (usually the right) and at a uniform height throughout the show. Each label should contain the name of the artist, the title, edition number (if applicable), year, and materials. Upscale galleries never put the price of the piece next to the work, so I don't do it either. Instead I design a price list on the computer, print from five to ten copies, and put each one inside a plastic sleeve. The price list should contain all the information on the labels, plus the size of the piece and the price. Viewers interested in buying work can carry a price list around with them as they view the show.

The reception. A successful reception is one at which everybody who comes has a wonderful time. In many ways it is like a party, but different in that, for you, it is a chance not only to bathe in the accolades showered upon you but also to do some serious networking.

Most receptions serve an alcoholic beverage, usually wine (presumably to lighten the atmosphere), and some sort of nonalcoholic beverage. Beyond that, anything goes; you can stop there or add a full buffet. You can make it simple by serving chips and dip, or go all out and hire a catering service. If you decide to serve food, make it finger food, since people will be carrying it around with them while they socialize. Don't serve messy food; you don't want it splattered on the art. Music creates a lively atmosphere, and live music can be an additional draw; but don't let the music overshadow the art or be too loud to allow conversation. You need to be able to communicate.

In addition to food and drink, you will need a table to serve it on, a tablecloth to make it look civilized, ice to keep the beverages cold,

I succeeded in simply attending as a spectator to the birth of all my works.
MAX ERNST

glasses, plates, tableware, serving utensils and bowls, napkins, and a trash can with lots of liners. You will also need people (other than exhibiting artists) to serve the drinks, put out the food, keep the food table tidy during the reception, and clear away the empty glasses.

You probably have friends who would be perfect for this job. It requires the type of person who wants to go to the reception to be supportive but isn't comfortable spending three hours standing around. This gives them something to do. If possible divide the job into shifts, with a bartender and a food monitor for the first half of the reception, and a second pair for the second half.

You should have someone, other than one of the artists, who is designated to handle sales during the reception. The artist's job is to welcome people to the opening, to discuss the art with them, and to stand around looking like a genius, *not* to soil his or her hands with things like money.

No, painting is not made to decorate apartments. It is an instrument of war, for attack and defense against the enemy.

PABLO PICASSO

Don't expect a lot of sales at the reception, people want to contemplate a work of art before they buy it. Before the show, purchase some red stick-on dots at a stationery store just in case; the sales coordinator can put them on the wall next to the work as pieces are sold. If you are feeling mischievous, place a red dot next to a few pieces even though they aren't really sold, or arrange to have a friend buy a piece during the opening so that people can see the dot actually going up. Sometimes seeing a red dot can cause a run on the market.

Be sure that anyone who buys a piece knows the work will remain on view until the exhibition is over. If a buyer insists on removing the work before the end of the show, put another piece in its place. An exhibition with pieces missing looks unprofessional and tends to make the viewer think more about what is missing than about the art that is there.

Place a guest book in a prominent location during the reception so that interested viewers can add their names to your mailing list. If possible, erect a small light table with slides of pieces not hung in the show so prospective collectors can view the full range of each artist's work. Several copies of the price list, artist bios, and statements should be placed inside plastic sleeves and available for people to carry with them as they tour the show.

How to behave at your art opening. Arrive early and plan to stay until the end. The opening of an exhibition of your art is not a time to be fashionably late. People are coming to see and meet you, and it can be very disappointing for them if you are not there. Art world professionals often try to attend many openings in an evening, and you don't want to miss the opportunity to connect with any of them.

Be friendly to people you don't know. Art openings are uncomfortable places for people who don't know anyone. Treat them like you would a stranger in your house. Sometimes, if artists are shy or nervous, they have a tendency to want to huddle with their friends all night. This makes it hard for others to approach you, and you run the risk of missing out on sales and other opportunities. Tell your friends you have to circulate.

If this is a group show, place yourself within eyesight of your own work. Don't hide around a corner somewhere feigning nonchalance. You want to watch the responses your work is receiving, and, more importantly, you need to be within reach when people want to meet you.

Help the other artists in the show. If you see someone looking at another artist's work, go over and tell them a little about the artist. Offer to introduce them. Often a viewer will be interested in a piece but is too shy or polite to hunt the artist down. Ask the other artists to do the same for you, too. This keeps the energy high and creates an atmosphere of excitement for the viewers as well as the artists.

Keep your drinking to a minimum. It may look like a party, but for you it's work and you need to have your wits about you. After all the work you have done to create this moment, don't ruin it by slobbering drunkenly over a prospective collector. Go out to dinner with your friends afterward. Then you can celebrate.

During the run of the show. Once the art is up and the party is over, put your feet up for a day if you wish, then prepare to get back to work. Now is a good time to follow up on leads generated at the opening and to arrange for people who couldn't attend the reception to see the work. If the show is in a café, you have a perfect excuse. Invite the person to dinner or drinks. You can have a relaxed social visit, surrounded by your art on display. If the show is in a gallery-type setting, arrange to meet the person there or, if they prefer to go alone, gently remind them of the show dates and then back off. Persistence is a good thing, pushiness is not.

When the show is over. Taking down the show is never as much fun as hanging it, but it goes faster. Once the work is down, check the walls for holes, scrapes, or other damage. The gallery owner will probably expect you to return the space to the condition in which you received it. This may mean spackling and painting the walls. Return the lighting fixtures to their original condition as well.

Don't forget to deliver the art pieces to collectors who bought them.

And pat yourself on the back for a job well done.

There is a vitality, a life force, a quickening that is translated through you into action, and because there is only one of you in all time, this expression is unique. And if you block it, it will never exist through any other medium and be lost. The world will not have it. It is not your business to determine how good it is; nor how valuable it is; nor how it compares with other expressions. It is your business to keep it yours clearly and directly, to keep the channel open. You do not even have to believe in yourself or your work. You have to keep open and aware directly to the urges that motivate YOU. Keep the channel open. No artist is pleased. There is no satisfaction whatever at any time. There is only a queer, divine dissatisfaction; a blessed unrest that keeps us marching and makes us more alive than the others.

AGNES DEMILLE TO MARTHA GRAHAM

CHAPTER EIGHT

Making Connections

Connecting with other human beings is really what your quest is about. Of course, you want to exhibit and sell your art and be acclaimed for your efforts, but the vehicle that will make all these dreams come true is your connection with others. Every achievement I have made with my art came not just from all the hard work I put into it, but because someone, somewhere, saw the work, liked it, and helped it to reach even more people. You can't have successful shows if there is no one to see them or no one to write about them. You can't have sales if there is no one to buy the art. At every point, you have to interact with others to make things happen.

I'm sure you have heard the phrase, "It's who you know that counts." Usually this is spoken disparagingly, with a shrug of the shoulders, by someone who feels he or she wasn't born into the right social circles. What isn't said is that you can know almost anyone you want to, with a little effort on your part. What also isn't said is that you never know which path will lead to the person who can help you nor, for that matter, who that person is.

The key is to meet new people with a pure heart. If you see yourself as a person in need and other people as possessing what you want, you will come off as a hustler. The people you meet won't want to have anything to do with you, and you won't like yourself very much either. If, instead, you set out on an adventure carrying art you believe in, and approach each new person with generosity, you will find your social and business circles growing.

One of the best ways to widen your circle of art-world connections and find new venues for exhibiting and selling your art is to take your work to a new city in search of opportunities to show it. Choose any city, national or international, with a large and active art community. Once you have decided on the town, there are three approaches you may take: the Best Way, the Second Best Way, and the Still Okay Plan.

The Best Way is to choose a new town—Chicago, for example— and go on a scouting mission to check out the lay of the land. While you are there, make a list of the exhibition spaces you find. Return home and write letters to all of them, reappearing in Chicago a month or so later with your art. The advantage to this plan is that you can weed out inappropriate places early, discover others that aren't listed in the guidebooks, and have twice the number of chances to interact with the people you meet.

The Second Best Way of approaching a city is to skip the scouting mission and go straight to the business of making appointments for showing your work. The disadvantage to this plan is that it will be a less-efficient, less-focused use of your time. You may have to waste a several days showing your work to people who won't be right for it, but serendipity has a way of coming to your aid when you need it. The advantage of this plan is that you only have to come up with travel expenses for one trip instead of two. This can be a big advantage if your bank account, or time, is limited.

The Still Okay Plan is to skip the travel altogether. The disadvantage of this plan is that you won't be able to see the exhibition spaces and meet the people face to face. This makes it harder to bond and more difficult to make decisions regarding individual spaces, but it is still okay. When employing this plan, use the telephone as much as possible and make your connections over the airwaves.

I'm going to describe the Best Way in detail, and you can choose the parts of the information that pertain to the approach you decide to use. Some of these ideas have already been covered in chapter four, but I am including it again in this chapter so that the information here is complete.

The Best Way to Approach a New City

The scouting mission. Before you embark on a scouting mission, scrutinize the August issue of *Art in America* for galleries that might be appropriate for your work. (Unfortunately, *Art in America* only lists American cities. For foreign locations, see suggestions in chapter five.) When you arrive in town, pick up a local gallery guide at the first space you visit and search it for additional names. Then take several days to scout the galleries, museums, and nonprofit spaces on the list. When you walk into the galleries, if you see art you like, don't keep it to yourself; tell the person at the desk how wonderful the work is and why you like it. You may find yourself engaged in a fascinating conversation. Use common sense about this; if the gallery person is busy with a client or on the phone, don't force an interaction.

Why talk to these people? First, it's fun. As an artist, you think about art all the time, and there is nothing more pleasurable than finding another soul who thinks about art, too. Second, if you find you connect with the person, it may lead to something else. Third, talking to the staff of a gallery is an excellent way to discover if their philosophy jives with yours. If so, the space may be a good choice for your follow-up trip.

While you are there, ask the gallery person how they prefer to be approached for show consideration. Mention that you are an artist and want to send slides. To whom should the packet be addressed? Introduce yourself to the person you are talking to (this is the beginning of Name Recognition!), ask his or her name in return, and thank them for their assistance. On rare occasions—very rare occasions—the gallery person may ask to see your work at that moment, so it is a good idea to carry a set of slides and a bio just in case.

Do not insist that the attendants look at your slides right then and there. Gallery people may appear to be doing nothing, but they are working hard to keep business booming (or they think they are, at any rate). They will not look favorably upon you if you force them to stop and pay attention to you. More importantly, they will not look favorably upon your work.

Another certain irritant for the gallery staff is for an artist to come into the gallery, drop off some slides, and then walk right out again without even stopping to glance at the art. If you are not interested enough in the gallery to look at the art, why should the gallery be interested in you?

Preparing for the business trip. Once you have completed your scouting mission, return home and plan your attack. Your first activity should be to write thank-you notes to all the people you met and had any real interaction with, preferably on a color postcard of your work (more Name Recognition). Then make a list of all the galleries, non-profit spaces, museums, and art consultants you would like to approach. Your second trip should be scheduled for a month to six weeks after the first, no longer or the people you met might forget who you are. Three weeks ahead, write to all the names on the list and enclose your packet. Use the cover-letter format I described in chapter two, but add a personal note reminding the people you met on the scouting trip about the encounter. Something like, "I was in your gallery last week, and you kindly showed me the Paul Klee drawings in the back room. As you suggested, I am sending a set of slides for your consideration." The point of the note is to remind them that they have met you, and that you felt it was a pleasant interaction. This can become the foundation for building a relationship.

Planning the business trip. While you can stay wherever you want on the scouting trip, your choice of lodging is important on the business trip. If you have friends or family members in the area, you might be

> *Before, I had no taste for anything. I was filled with indifference toward everything that people wanted me to do. But the moment I had this box of colors in my hands, I had the feeling that my life was there.*
>
> HENRI MATISSE

tempted to stay with them to save hotel costs, but there are two disadvantages to this. The main disadvantage is the telephone. You will need a phone that you can use for an hour or two every day without infringing on the rights of your host. This phone line has to remain open during the day in case the people who received your packets try to make contact. There should be a recording device on the phone to avoid the mixed-up or partial information that can result if your friends' children try to take a message while you are out. Another downside to staying with friends is that after a few hours of marching from gallery to gallery, your feet will hurt, your emotions will be played out, the adrenaline you have been running on will desert you, and you will be in immediate need of a soft bed where you can put your feet up and zone out. If you are sleeping on someone's couch in the living room, you will soon be in a state of advanced exhaustion. If cost is an issue, consider sharing the trip with another artist. Sharing the experience with someone else, someone who is also courageously putting art out there, can make it much more pleasurable.

You don't have to stay at a hotel, just someplace private and close to the action. When I go to New York, I sublease an apartment in Soho from a friend. People going on vacation are often looking for someone to sublease their places; you can discover them through local newspapers and art magazines.

What to bring. Imagine ahead of time what it will be like to carry your work from gallery to gallery, open up your portfolio, and show it to people in places where you have no control over the circumstances in which it will be seen. Obviously you want to control as many of the variables as possible.

The first is transportation. If you are traveling to a large city like New York, expect to do a lot of walking. Gallery districts can go on for blocks and blocks. You can take the subway or a taxi to different areas of town such as Soho or Uptown, but within an area hiring a taxi isn't practical. I strap my portfolio to a small handcart and drag it happily behind me. The cart can become unwieldy when climbing more than a few stairs, so I avoid the subway.

When I am traveling to a town like Dallas, where everything is spread out, I rent a car to carry my work. Since it is easy to drive right up to most galleries and museums, I don't always need my luggage cart, but I keep it in the car, just in case.

In Paris, neither a car nor the cart is all that practical. Even if I ignore the fact that driving in a foreign country makes me a nervous wreck, it is impossible to find parking anywhere near the places I want to go. So I bring plenty of taxi money and, because one often has to walk long distances, my trusty cart. But Paris is covered with cobblestones (charming at any other time) and filled with buildings completed before elevators were invented. I often end up carrying my cart as much as I pull it. So, when choosing a handcart for your trip, consider its weight as much as its load-carrying ability.

The second thing to consider is which art to bring and how to protect it. The carrying case should be easy to open, and it should show your work to its best advantage. For small works on paper, such as drawings or photographs, a large black portfolio case (such as the kind available from the Light Impressions catalog) full of matted prints can create a professional impression. Avoid those portfolio cases with binder rings and plastic pages. Placing almost any work of art inside those plastic sheets will make it look cheesy. Besides, you don't want to mimic a traveling salesman. Consider getting a clamshell portfolio (one that opens completely flat), so that you can present the art easily without removing it from the portfolio. Before you purchase any portfolio case, hold it by the handle to see how it fits your body. It should clear the floor when you are holding it. If you have to bend your elbow to carry the case, your arm will grow very tired. If the finished size of your art measures 11" x 14", purchase a 16" x 20" portfolio case, then matte each piece to fit. Use two-ply matting board (archival, of course) rather than the usual four-ply board. Since two-ply board is thinner, you can fit more art into the portfolio while carrying around less weight.

Pay special attention to the sequencing of your art. Place your strongest images first to capture your viewer's attention, followed by the rest, then finish with another dynamite piece. Of course, all of your pieces should be your best. Never include work you don't feel able to defend wholeheartedly, but within that category there are always a few that stand out. The portfolio should carry fifteen to twenty pieces, rarely more; otherwise you may lose the attention of your

You shouldn't say it is not good. You should say you do not like it; and then, you know, you're perfectly safe.

JAMES McNEILL WHISTLER

viewer. Always leave them wanting more, rather than saturated by the ordeal. When you sequence the work, pay attention to the effect each piece has on the one next to it, since that is the way they will be seen. Rearrange them until you have the strongest possible line-up.

If you create large paintings, sculptures, or installation work, your preparation will be more challenging. Most galleries want to see at least one actual piece of art. I know painters who have traveled successfully by removing their canvases from the stretcher bars, rolling them up, and carrying them inside cardboard or plastic (lighter!) tubes they have fashioned with a shoulder strap. Shoulder straps are something to look for in any carrying case. You never know when you will need your hands free.

Artists whose work will not travel—sculptors and installation artists, for example—will need to create presentation materials to convey the power of the work. Possible choices might be a mock-up (a portable version of the piece), drawings showing the piece installed, a computer rendition of the work, or 4" x 5", or maybe even 8" x 10" color transparencies of actual pieces. If you bring large transparencies, invest in a portable light table (battery-powered) for viewing them. You don't want to rely on the light sources at the gallery. A CD-ROM can present your work beautifully, but you are limited to the availability and sophistication of the computers you find at the galleries you visit. Even if you carry your own laptop for viewing the CD-ROM, you may encounter people who have an aversion to computers. Forget about putting your work on video unless it is absolutely necessary; most galleries will not bother looking at tapes.

Regardless of the kind of art you make, pay as much attention to the presentation of your work as you do to your art. Present yourself as the professional you hope to be. Everything should be designed to be easy to handle, since looking at your portfolio should be a positive experience for the viewer. Bring lots of extra sets of slides, bios, statements, and business cards for giving to gallery personnel who ask for them.

You will need a combination appointment book, address book, and notebook containing the names, addresses, and phone numbers of the people you intend to approach. Because I don't like to carry around a lot of extra paper, I buy a tiny three-ring binder with alphabetical divisions especially for the trip. At the top of each page, I list the name of a gallery and its address and phone, leaving the rest of the page empty for making notes after I have contacted them. If you want to be really thorough, copy the information straight out of your *Art in America Gallery Guide* (perhaps reduced to 50 percent) and paste it to the top of your notebook page. In the front of my notebook, I put a calendar so that I can keep track of appointments. Take extra paper in order to add more names as you go.

In my ever-zealous quest to carry as little as possible, I bought a watch that was touted to have the ability to contain a hundred phone numbers and a hundred pages of notes. I thought it would be the perfect way to dispense with carrying an appointment book, but now I think I may have gone too far. Those little bitty alphabet letters take hours to input and retrieve. I do use the watch for phone numbers (it is handy having it right on my arm), but I still carry my little notebook for more detailed information like business notes and appointments.

Bringing a small phone answering machine is a great idea if you will be staying at a place that has a phone but no reliable method for recording phone messages. If you are staying at a hotel this won't be necessary since many hotels have voicemail, but check ahead to be sure.

When you arrive. The first thing to do is install your telephone answering machine. Then start calling the names on your list for appointments. Your inclination may be to put this off, but don't give in to that. The demands on your time will increase as the trip advances. By the end of the expedition, you will be wishing you had just a few more days to follow up new leads you have generated.

Those dreaded follow-up phone calls. Thank God for the telephone! You pick up the ear piece, dial the phone number of a prospective gallery, and say, "Hi! I'm Earnest Artist. I'm a painter from Miami, and I sent you slides last week along with a letter saying I would be in town for ten days. Do you remember receiving them? You do?! Yes, the paintings with snow on the palm trees! Right! And angels on rollerblades, yes! You hated them? Oh."

Praise the Lord for the telephone! Because of this miracle of

No one can make you feel inferior without your consent.

ELEANOR ROOSEVELT

technology, you were able to experience this less-than-perfect moment from the comfort of your hotel room. This is far better than trudging to the gallery, portfolio strapped to your back, and being told the news to your reddened face, perhaps even in front of witnesses. And because you were miles away, stretched out on the bed, you were relaxed enough to turn this apparent disaster into a triumph, "I'm sorry the work isn't right for you, but thank you for being so candid. I wonder, do you know anyone in town who might be interested in this work? The Snow Palm Gallery? What is the phone number? And who should I ask for? Terrific! Thank you."

The next step is a piece of cake. Why? Because within five minutes, in the midst of being rejected, you bagged yourself the most coveted of prizes, a promising lead. Now all you have to do is call the Snow Palm Gallery. "Hi! I'm Earnest Artist. David Dope, of the David Dope Gallery, suggested that you might be interested in my work...," and you are in the door.

Of course, not all of your attempts to connect will work out happily. Expect about a 10 percent positive response rate. At every opportunity, ask for suggestions and follow them up. The names in your address book should begin to multiply. Don't forget to ask for names in all the categories of art professionals you want to meet, including art consultants, museum curators, directors of nonprofit spaces, magazine editors, and private dealers, as well as gallery owners.

Presenting your portfolio. Start with the assumption that the person who has agreed to see you may only spare you ten minutes to present your work. He or she may wave you into a room the size of a closet with papers piled high on the desk and say, "So, let's see it." This usually doesn't happen, but be prepared for it anyway. Bring everything you need to present the work at its best in the shortest amount of time. If the work is small enough, say matted drawings, consider carrying it in a clamshell portfolio (one that opens completely flat) so that you can handle the works in their own pristine environment, thus avoiding the cluttered desk. If you are showing transparencies, carry a small, portable light table that runs on batteries. (You can't be sure there will be an available electrical outlet.) Avoid covering the art with plastic bags or slip sheets if you can, unless it is absolutely necessary

*I never got a job
I didn't create
for myself.*
RUTH GORDON

for protection. Removing and replacing slip sheets can waste a lot of time.

I always carry a stack of bios, statements, slides, and reviews in my carrying case. When I open the case, I hand a bio to the client, giving them something to look at while I unpack my art. I place the work in a stack facing the client, and then I watch for clues. Most people want to look at the art at their own pace. Unless they are handling my art with a lighted cigarette in one hand and are swirling a glass of bourbon with the other, I let them do it.

I usually start out by telling them a little about the work, a sentence or two describing my process and concerns with the work. Then I shut up and let them look. They will either start talking themselves, ask me questions, or look at the work in silence. What I am doing at this point is matching my energy to theirs. There is nothing more futile than trying to communicate with someone when you are both trying to talk at once, or when one person is thinking at racetrack speed and the other person's brain is lying in the sun. When I walk into the room, I drop whatever level of energy I happen to be carrying (which is usually panic energy) and allow myself to settle into the other person's speed. This has the added advantage of taking my attention off of myself and directing it toward someone else, and soon I forget to be nervous.

The person to whom you are showing the work may be the kind of person who likes to do the talking. You can learn a lot from listening. Sometimes the responses can be very insightful, sometimes they reflect more about what they had for breakfast then anything having to do with your art. Pay attention and file the information away for later contemplation. If you get the same response from several people, it is time to start taking it seriously. I have shown my portfolio hundreds of times, and my experience has been that when one person picks out three pieces because they are so good, the next person will pull out the same three because they are so bad. Over the years, it has gotten to the point that I can almost tell which art school someone attended, and their year of graduation, by which pieces of my work he or she likes.

Sometimes the person wants to hear you talk and will ask you questions about the work, or mention other artists who work in the same vein and ask you what you think of them. If you have a

No opinion, however absurd and incredible, can be imagined, which has not been maintained by one of the philosophers.

RENÉ DESCARTES

background in art history, or if you spend a lot of time attending galleries and museums, you will probably know who they are talking about. You *should* know who they are talking about. You should also know how their work differs from yours and be able to discuss that.

I have an exercise I give in class called "Your Place in Art History" to prepare students for this kind of situation. Each student is required to research where their own art fits into art history for an oral presentation to the class. They are asked to include the movement or tradition from which their work stems (for example, German expressionism), define the main thrust of the movement in a sentence or two, then name three artists from that time period whose work can be seen as antecedent and three contemporary artists whose work can be compared to their own. For this exercise to be useful, the artists you research must have a direct relationship to your art; they should not be drawn from a list of random artists you admire.

Another thing you can do for yourself is to rehearse the presentation of your portfolio with a friend, encouraging them to ask you questions about the art so that you can practice formulating your answers.

Sometimes the gallery person just wants to look at the work in silence. You can usually recognize this type of person when they grunt dismissively every time you open your mouth to talk. This is your cue to shut up. Try not to take it personally. These people come from the school of thought that believes art must speak for itself. They want a private experience with the work. Let them have it.

After you return home. Write follow-up letters to everyone you met, thanking them for their time and attention. If they said or did something that was particularly meaningful to you, let them know it. If you spent two weeks in a city and met with thirty or so art professionals, you should have returned with at least one positive response, probably more. Regardless of how many actual commitments you bagged, remember that your real purpose was to plant the seeds for future relationships, and you did that admirably. It may not have been easy schlepping your art from place to place, but you did it!

Now begins the process of courting your contacts. Put their names and addresses on your mailing list, and every time your art is in an

One thinks like a hero to behave like a merely decent human being.

MAY SARTON

exhibition, large or small, send them an announcement. If they are even mildly interested in your work, their interest will grow. One of my former students, photographer Frank Yamrus, has used this approach successfully in dealing with prospective galleries as his career progressed.

Unaware that I knew Frank, a San Francisco art dealer was praising his method of approaching her. Apparently Frank had sent her a packet some time earlier with the usual set of slides, bio, and statement. She glanced at them, thought they were moderately interesting, and returned them in the SASE he had provided. I don't think she even included any kind of letter when she returned the work. Frank dutifully added her name to his mailing list and sent her an announcement whenever his work was exhibited, expecting nothing in return. The gallery owner saw the postcards, looked at the images of his work, and became more interested with each mailing she received. When Frank had completed a new body of work, he again sent a slide packet to the gallery. This time she looked it over with interest. Although she eventually decided against adding him to her stable (his work didn't quite fit the gallery's focus), she has taken an interest in his career and when an opportunity arises to recommend his work, she happily does so.

Relationships, of any kind, don't happen overnight. With every new contact you make you are creating the beginning of a new association. Don't expect instant results. You are in this for the long term.

Skipping all that travel and planning your campaign from home. If you are unable to undertake all the travel just described, start out by choosing a city to approach, just like you would have above. When you make your list of targets, be as all-inclusive as you can. Your list should be anywhere from twenty to eighty names long. Don't just find the names of one or two galleries and send your slides to them, thinking you will find others if they reject you. This is the surest way to court heartbreak, because you will become invested in their acceptance. The days will drag by as you wait for their answer, becoming increasingly nervous over the outcome. No, no, no, *mon cher*! Don't do this to yourself. You are not a wallflower hoping against hope that someone will show pity and dance with you. You are a brilliant artist

I always have the impression that the work is apprentice work, and that if I can just finish it, then I'll really do something good.
SUSAN SONTAG

in charge of your life. Send out twenty packets at once to the top names on your list. When one packet is returned, put a check by the name and send the slides out again to the next person on the list. Simple. Easy. Professional.

As an excuse to make verbal contact with the people to whom you are sending slides, and also to expedite matters, telephone the gallery a few days after they have received them. Ask whomever answers the phone if the slides have arrived. If the person is not sure, describe the work to prompt their memory. See if you can engage the person in conversation: "Does the packet seem to be in order? Did you address it to the right person? Does the work seem like it might be right for the gallery? If it is not right for them, do they have any suggestions for you? What is the name of the person you are talking to?" Don't be a pest, of course, just make contact. If the person wants to chat, so much the better. Keep notes while you are talking, writing down any business information they might give you as well as any personal comments. If the person you are talking to says he or she won't be able to attend to your slides until after returning from a vacation in Bermuda, make a note of it. The next time you talk, ask them how the trip went.

I remember one January when I was filled with the urge to sweep my life clean, as I do every year at that time. That particular year, I was irritated that over a hundred sets of slides had been out in the world for some time. I was tired of it. I wanted them back. I went down my list of delinquent slide returners and started calling. "Hi. My name is Cay Lang. I sent a packet of slides to you eight months ago and received no reply in return. I wonder if you could locate them and send them back. Yes, I will wait while you look in your files." By the fifth call, I got lucky. The receptionist found the slides and liked them. She asked if she could keep them one more day to show to her boss. I generously acquiesced. The gallery ended up selling over fifty photographs to one of its clients, enough to fill the top two floors of his skyscraper in New York.

Never explain—your friends do not need it and your enemies will not believe you anyway.

ELBERT HUBBARD

Other Ways of Connecting

Entering the art world through the side door. One of the best ways to become part of the art scene is to volunteer to help at a nonprofit art space, museum, or art gallery. With the funding cutbacks of the nineties, these institutions are often understaffed and the people overworked. Decide how much time you can give, then telephone the art space of your choice and ask for the volunteer coordinator. Even if you can only be there every other Thursday, the little you do can make a big difference to the organization. It may need help with fund raising, hanging exhibitions, membership or any of a thousand other details. The advantages for you are many. You will learn behind-the-scenes information about how the art world works. You will forge relationships with other art professionals in an atmosphere of dedication to a cause worth fighting for. You will gain respect and gratitude from the staff members. And later on, if there is a chance for them to help you out, they will be thrilled to do so because they know you to be a committed artist. Don't expect them to give you a show, however, as this could be seen as a compromise to their integrity. What they can do is keep an eye out in the larger art community and, when an opportunity arises, put your name forward. This is a big thing. In the art world, word travels quickly. Conversely, if you don't live up to your commitments, such as not showing up to hang a show, those words travel quickly, too. When you agree to help an organization, keep your word.

Enthusiasm is the electricity of life. How do you get it? You act enthusiastic until you make it a habit.

GORDON PARKS

Attending gallery openings. Most galleries hold an opening reception for each new exhibition. Attending these events can be a great way to learn more about the structure of the art world as well as provide a fine opportunity for networking. When you go to an art opening, pay attention to everything—the art, of course, and the way the show is hung; but also the people. See if you can tell by the way a person is dressed which part of the art world he represents. Who are the artists? The gallery owners? The critics? The collectors? If you like the show, introduce yourself to the artist and the gallery director and congratulate them on the installation. The amount of mingling you do is entirely up to you. If you are the kind of person who likes meeting new people, art openings can be a lot of fun. If you are shy, go anyway and participate as much or as little as feels right to you. If any particular gallery consistently shows work that you feel is in alignment with your own artistic direction, make a point of attending all the openings. The gallery owner will notice and be appreciative and, when you are ready to present your work to them, be more likely to give you a chance.

Using your Aunt Emma's contacts. You may have an influential family member or friend who wants to help with your career. Maybe your aunt plays bridge with the director of the local museum. This is wonderful, and when she offers to telephone the director on your behalf say "Yes! Thank you!" But you need to understand, even if Aunt Emma does not, that her influence may get you in the door, but nothing more is guaranteed. If a gallery director wants to maintain a reputation for integrity, he or she can't give exhibitions to relatives or friends unless those relatives or friends have already gained some reputation as artists. If the director compromises this policy, his or her own career could go down the tubes. But a person in that position can look at your work, make suggestions, and, on occasion, if the work fits with the mandate of the museum, do more than that.

Applying for a residency at an art colony. A short period spent at an art colony can be a wonderful experience on many levels. The most obvious is the fact that you are given room and board and a studio and nothing is expected of you in return except that you make art. What isn't mentioned is that a residency can provide an intense bonding experience with other artists. Being removed from the demands of your real life, stimulated by the thrill of making art all day (usually in a beautiful setting), and surrounded by other artists who are experiencing the same thing can create a deep connection. To receive a residency at an artist colony (like the MacDowell Colony or the Djerassi Foundation, for instance) you must submit an application for consideration. Although the competition is steep, winners are chosen for their art rather than for their résumé, which means beginners have a chance, but be aware that it may not happen instantly since many art colonies have a several-year waiting list. Some of the artists you meet there will have established international careers, others were chosen (like you) just because they make amazing art. I have listed some well-known artist colonies in the appendix.

> *Artistic growth is, more than anything else, a refining of the sense of truthfulness. The stupid believe that to be truthful is easy: only the great artist knows how difficult it is.*
> WILLA CATHER

Hiring a publicist. In the last few years, it has become increasingly popular for artists to hire publicists to help put their name before the public. This can be a costly enterprise, and although it has worked well for some artists, it can just as easily backfire. If you are considering doing this, be very careful who you decide to hire. The publicist needs to understand not only how to get media attention, but how to do it without sounding the red alarm along the backyard fence of the art world. If people in the art world think you are more concerned with gaining attention than making art, they will dismiss you at once; and once people in the art world start thinking of an artist as a hustler, they start devaluing the art. If you are shopping around for a publicist, try to find one who has proven himself by working for other successful artists.

Becoming an art writer. This path may not be for everyone, but for those people who can combine a love of writing with a love of art, becoming an art writer is guaranteed to connect you with art-world inner circles. People may not always like art critics, but they invite them to all of their parties. Gallery owners, nonprofit-space curators, and museum directors all know that if they want the public to attend their events, they need to get coverage in the local media. So if you are an art writer, the galleries will court you. What a nice change from being an artist, where you have to court the galleries. The downside is that once you have become defined as a critic, it is often difficult for the art world to accept that you are also an artist. It is not an insurmountable obstacle, but the art writers I know who are also artists all complain about it.

If you decide to do this, don't do it just for the perks. Becoming a writer takes as much commitment and hard work as becoming an artist. The impulse should come from within. To begin, telephone an art publication that runs regular reviews of exhibitions (like *Artweek* or the *New Art Examiner*) and ask for writing guidelines. Most publications will tell you to write a sample review and mail it to them. If they like it, they will either print it or give you another assignment, and you are on your way. Eventually they will send you a check for your efforts. When you open it, you will understand why critics always have that lean and hungry look. They are outrageously underpaid.

Authors are sometimes like tomcats: they distrust all the other toms, but they are kind to the kittens.

MALCOLM COWLEY

CHAPTER NINE

Helpful Hints

I call this chapter Helpful Hints, but I think of the information it contains as more along the lines of ways of thinking that are absolutely
essential. Throughout the book you have absorbed information on
how the art world works and the ways in which it is changing, meth-
ods for creating a professional artist's packet, criteria for planning
a career strategy and carrying it out, the best ways of dealing with

galleries and exhibitions, suggestions for streamlining your office, directions for staging an exhibition from beginning to end, and the development of networking skills. All that is terrific, but it is just information. Information is important, but it won't take you very far without tenacity and an open mind and heart.

▬▬▬▬ Creating Your Own Art Community

One way you can help yourself keep on track is to create a support group with other like-minded artists. I don't mean a loose friends-support-friends kind of association. What I am talking about is a group of artists who have come together for the specific purpose of helping each other launch (or resume) their careers. One of the reasons my six-month class works is that the students come with a high level of commitment and a willingness to work at a brisk pace. Each week we deal with a different aspect of the problem (for example, writing a statement or setting goals) and we don't move on until everyone is up to speed. Peer-group pressure can work wonders in your life. You will find yourself dealing with things you have been putting off for years rather than having to face the group with some lame excuse like, "I would have brought my statement but the baby threw up on it."

The focus of the group should be clear to everyone involved. The group I am suggesting is really a business group, where members report on their business activities at each meeting, and offer and receive help and suggestions from the others in turn. Another more traditional type of artists' group is a critique group, which is designed to discuss the art itself. Or you can create a hybrid of the two.

You can use this book as your outline for setting weekly agendas. Why not produce a group show as well? I can guarantee that the members will surpass themselves to get the work done. Who wants to risk screwing up an exhibition with their entire social circle in attendance? The prospect of public humiliation can be a big motivator; it has worked for me on many occasions.

The group should meet regularly, with not too much time between meetings. I like a weekly format; things move fast enough for you to

Life shrinks
or expands in
proportion to
one's courage.
ANAÏS NIN

That ripoff Kosuth!
I thought of it first!
WILLIAM WEGMAN

feel your life changing, but not so fast that you can't keep up. Group dynamics are different in every circle, but there are a few pitfalls that seem to occur in almost every group.

When you change your life in this way, it can bring up a lot of fears and free-wheeling emotions. Be careful that the group doesn't degenerate into a therapy session. Create an agreement with each other that you will concentrate on business goals; personal problems can be dealt with elsewhere. It is okay to acknowledge that life is difficult and people have problems, then immediately move on to the project at hand. If you don't, you will find the group falling apart in a few weeks because the members feel frustrated that nothing is getting done.

Also, fear and anxiety have a tendency to be catching. You can't help feeling anxious, but you can control what you do about it. Instead of allowing those emotions to fester, realize that inventing failure scenarios is your psyche's way of trying to make sure that nothing changes. Your insecurities will do everything they can to convince you that some external person or thing is the real source of the problem. Anxiety and excitement are two faces of the same kind of highly-charged energy. Choose excitement instead.

Another problem that seems to recur is a marked difference in each person's comfort with speaking in the group. Some people never say anything, and others won't shut up. This can drive everyone crazy. There is an easy way to deal with this. Buy a wind-up kitchen timer and give each person exactly ten minutes as you go around the circle making reports on what you have done. Don't miss anyone. Every week, every person should have a chance to speak. Do this from the first meeting, so that everyone accepts it as a given. If you wait until you have a problem, the big talker in your group will become insulted, then you will all have to talk about it even more.

The group should number no more than twelve, and ten is ideal. In a group this size, every person should have enough time each week to deal with the things they need to deal with. A typical meeting should last no more than three hours. Choose the members of the group carefully. Look for a certain level of competence in the art; you can't market work that isn't ready. Look for commitment and a willingness to work hard. Look for emotional stability. And look for people you want to spend time with.

Keep away from people who try to belittle your ambitions. Small people always do that, but the really great make you feel that you, too, can become great.

MARK TWAIN

If you live in an isolated area or have recently moved to a new town, you may not know enough artists to start a group. Don't be shy. Put an ad in the local paper, hang flyers in the art department at the local college, try the community art gallery. You will be amazed how many other artists feel isolated too, even in urban areas. Even if you can only locate one other person, if it is the right person whole new worlds can open up.

Regardless of whether you are working with other artists or by yourself, there are certain beliefs and attitudes that are essential for living a full and successful life as an artist. Don't shortchange yourself in these areas; your outlook on life is what it is all about.

> *A man can fail many times, but he isn't a failure until he begins to blame somebody else.*
>
> JOHN BURROUGHS

Absolutely Essential Ways of Thinking

The art always comes first. It is easy to lose sight of this when you become embroiled in the demands of business. The truth is that, without the art, there can be no business. Remember that it is the work that counts most, and allow nothing to leave your studio before it meets your standards. Your career as an artist will be based on the quality of your art, and the quickest way to end a career is to send out work that isn't ready.

Make the best art you can, then push yourself further. An artist is always in the process of becoming. If you find yourself repeating past successes, making the same painting over and over, or painting to please your friends or your dealer, you are probably avoiding the next step in your growth.

Develop regular work habits. It's great if you can get to the studio every day, but it is not necessary. What is necessary is to maintain regular work habits. Every time you quit working on your art for any period of time, you have to undergo the agony of getting started again. Resuming art production when you haven't attended to it for a while is not just the simple act of picking up a paintbrush. (Actually it is, but it doesn't feel like it.) You have to go through all the emotional roadblocks you have created for yourself before you can get there, which can be very convoluted. You have to carve time out of the other demands and interests that have moved into your life, and those other things will not go meekly. Once you have achieved regular work habits, hang onto them fiercely. Even if you have a limited time to work, once your mind accepts that every Saturday and Sunday afternoon it will get to think about art, it will begin to jump immediately to the point where you left off last time. This means the art continues to get deeper each time you work.

Get a studio. It doesn't have to be glamorous, it just has to be yours. The basic requirements for an artist's studio are privacy and the freedom to make a mess and leave it there. Working on the dining room table until the kids come home just does not cut it. You need to leave your art out so that you can pick up where you left off. You need to be able to see the work fresh the next day. You also need the freedom to make mistakes without anyone else seeing them. Without these things, the work will not grow. If necessary, declare your studio off-limits to your loved ones. An artist needs to have a place where he or she can be free from judgment, no matter how well-meaning.

Mixed-media artist Sas Colby offers some tips for protecting the sanctity of your studio. She marks her planned studio days on the calendar so that she doesn't inadvertently double-book her time. She is careful never to invite anyone to meet her there, and adamant that no phone be installed. When she arrives at the studio, she is ready to work, secure in the fact that she won't be interrupted.

If you can't afford to rent a studio separate from your house, perhaps you have some options you haven't considered. A spare bedroom or garage can work. Maybe you have a friend with extra space. Is there an empty building that has gone unrented in your town? Perhaps the owner will let you use it in exchange for watering the lawn, or a free painting, or token rent. Occupied buildings are more attractive to prospective purchasers. Your presence alone could be enough payment. Look around you. You have more options than you think.

Learn to balance your life and your art. This is the real trick to living your life as an artist. Without your art, your life won't be full. Without a life, your art will become stale. Realize from the beginning that you are here for the duration. Treat all the components of your life—your family, your friends, your work—as gifts. It may not be easy, but you will find room for them all. But make sure that the things you give time to are of your own choosing rather than done to meet someone else's expectations. There *is* time in your life for everything that you care about, but not for everything that everyone else cares about. You have to be the protector of your time.

Beware of destructive assumptions. The art world, just like any other subculture, is full of widely-held beliefs about itself. One particularly insidious belief is that it is almost impossible for an artist to (*fill in any goal*: find a gallery, get a show, sell his or her art, get an appointment with a museum curator).

Where do people get these ideas? And why do they hang on to them?

Guess what: It isn't brain surgery. Having an active career as an artist is only hard if you decide it is going to be hard. You could just as readily decide it is easy. It could be exciting. It could be enlightening. It could be a chance to learn something new. Climbing a mountain is climbing a mountain. It takes effort, but so does everything else. Besides, you know it can't be all that hard, because look how many other people have already done it.

There was a woman on the radio who was being interviewed because she had just completed building a log cabin all by herself. She taught herself how to do it. It took her three years working on weekends and after work. The interviewer was amazed that anyone would spend that much time building a house, but the woman answered, "I had a choice. I could work for three years and end up with a log cabin, or I could not work on it for three years and not have one. Either way I would be putting in the same amount of time."

Watch out for midcareer bitterness. Taking a passive attitude toward your career can result in a bitterness that can eat you up and take all the joy out of everything, including making art. This phenomenon occurs when an artist despairs because his or her career hasn't gone as far or as fast as expected. Here the artist is, after all these years of slaving away in the studio, and nothing to show for it. Maybe he or she got

If it looks like art, chances are it is somebody else's art.
ATTRIBUTED TO CHUCK CLOSE BY ERIC FISCHL

a little attention early on and then *pouf!*, it all just disappeared. It's not that the artist isn't talented, or dedicated; often the artist is both. Bitterness is a result of thinking the world is supposed to come to you, but it really doesn't work that way. Remember my friend who waited patiently in her second-floor apartment for her White Knight until she realized that his horse wouldn't fit in the elevator? Like her, you have to go outside to meet him.

And you have to be methodical and thorough. You have to be prepared to go out and look for him every day until the job is done, no matter how long it takes. There is nothing more discouraging than making a half-hearted attempt at handling your career. It gives you the illusion that you tried and failed, when really you never tried at all.

Bitterness is a choice, not a reality. It is the choice of the passive. Another choice is to take action. People who take action feel powerful, and people who feel powerful become powerful.

More on midcareer bitterness. Sometimes the bad taste in your mouth is a result of disappointment with the art world itself. When you chose to be an artist, it was partly because you thought that here was one career that was free from self-interest; a place where people cared about the more important things. Then you became involved with the art world and discovered that it could be just as corrupt as anywhere else. In a way, the art world is more corrupt than, say, the business world, because at least people in the business world admit that they are motivated by self-interest. For me, this was a horrifying realization. I wanted to be an artist because I felt it was a grander, cleaner place to be. When I discovered that the art world was a tiny neighborhood full of power-plays and intrigues, I was brokenhearted. Eventually I came to accept that the full range of human nature will play itself out in any arena. The art world may be small, but it is large enough to attract every type of human being.

The other thing I came to realize is that the art itself really is what I thought it was: clean and grand. One hour in the studio will remind you of this. Creating art is a search for truth, and viewing art can be a catalyst for profound understanding. Art will always be larger than any social group who claims it. If the thought of participating in the mainstream art world makes your flesh crawl, don't do it. Make your art for the rest of the world, skip the gallery system, and show your art on your own terms.

There really is enough to go around. There is an intelligence in the universe that favors life. This intelligence wants you to succeed. Many people in the art world carry an attitude of scarcity. *There aren't enough galleries; there aren't enough showing spaces; there aren't enough opportunities.* This attitude only creates more scarcity.

Reality will mold itself to fit your expectations. I know this is contrary to many people's beliefs, but I have seen the proof of it endless times in my classes. The artist who comes to the program with an attitude of adventure, a belief in the ability to succeed, and a willingness to do the work finds triumph after triumph. The artist who comes with the attitude that the work is too hard, that success is almost impossible, and that the competition is too steep will find those expectations realized as well. This artist will have successes, but only moderate ones, intermittently realized, which is exactly what was expected. The universe has given each artist a personally tailored version of success.

> *There is nothing fiercer than a failed artist. The energy remains, but, having no outlet, it implodes in a great black fart of rage which smokes up all the inner windows of the soul.*
>
> ERICA JONG

If you find it difficult to accept this idea, then I offer an experiment for you to try. For six months, do the work wholeheartedly, and if you can't actually believe that the universe wants you to succeed, pretend that you do. Whenever you start to feel that your task is impossible, remind yourself that, for right now, the task is easy and exciting. When people ask you how you are doing, say "Great! This isn't nearly as hard as I thought." Every letter you write, every action you take should carry that attitude of conviction. It won't be long before you'll find that you aren't pretending anymore. You will be too busy keeping up with your show commitments.

Attitude is everything. My life isn't always perfect, sometimes it seems to drag along forever with nothing good ever happening. Sometimes I buy into it and think, *Life is the pits, and it will never get any better.* This can go on for months, years, at a time. Then one morning I wake up and wonder, could I have been contributing to the creation of that reality just by reinforcing it with my thoughts? I change my attitude, and before long, my external experiences alter themselves to match. That doesn't mean you can avoid life's tragedies by wishing them away; it means you can add to life's bonuses by expecting them as well. It also doesn't mean that thoughts are the only thing that count, actions are important too. You still have to work.

I have noted that, barring accidents, artists whose powers wear best and last longest are those who have trained themselves to work under adversity. Great artists treasure their time with a bitter and snarling miserliness.

CATHERINE DRINKER BOWEN

Don't be afraid to make mistakes. You'll make them no matter how carefully you plan anyway. Look at those little errors in judgment as part of the package and cut yourself some slack. Sometimes your mistakes will lead to a better place than the one you had in mind. Jim Pomeroy, a brilliant performance artist, used to say to his students, "To be an artist you have to make five hundred mistakes, so you might as well get started."

Oh yeah, and have fun!

I think I'm beginning to learn something about it.

AUGUSTE RENOIR

[His last words about painting, at age seventy-eight]

*A*ppendices

Books of Interest to Artists

Art Theory, History, and Gossip

Atkins, Robert, ed. *Art Speak: A Guide to Modern Ideas, Movements, and Buzzwords.* New York: Abbeville Press, 1990.

————. *Art Spoke: A Guide to Modern Ideas, Movements, and Buzzwords, 1848–1944.* New York: Abbeville Press, 1993.

Barnet, Sylvan. *A Short Guide to Writing About Art.* Boston: Little Brown and Company, 1981.

De Coppet, Laura, and Alan Jones. *The Art Dealers.* New York: Clarkson N. Potter Inc, 1984.

Gablik, Suzi. *The Reenchantment of Art.* New York: Thames and Hudson, 1991.

Haden-Guest, Anthony. *True Colors.* New York: The Atlantic Monthly Press, 1996.

Hauser, Arnold. *The Social History of Art.* New York: Vintage Books, 1958, reissued 1985.

Hoving, Thomas. *Making the Mummies Dance.* New York: Simon and Schuster, 1993.

Rose, Barbara, ed. *Art as Art: The Selected Writings of Ad Reinhardt.* Berkeley and Los Angeles: University of California Press, 1991.

Weschler, Lawrence. *Shapinsky's Karma, Bogg's Bills, and Other True Life Tales.* New York: Penguin Books, 1988.

Wolfe, Tom. *The Painted Word.* New York: Bantam Books, 1975.

Creative Inspiration

Bayles, David, and Ted Orland. *Art & Fear: Observations on the Perils (and Rewards) of Artmaking.* Santa Barbara: Capra Press, 1993.

Cameron, Julia: *The Artist's Way. A Spiritual Path to Higher Creativity.* New York: Tarcher/Pedigree Books, 1992.

Edwards, Betty. *Drawing on the Artist Within.* New York: Simon and Schuster, 1987.

———. *Drawing on the Right Side of the Brain.* Los Angeles: J. P. Tarcher, Inc., 1979.

Flack, Audrey. *Art & Soul: Notes on Creating.* New York: Penguin Books, 1991.

Goldberg, Natalie. *Writing Down the Bones.* Boston: Shambhala Publications, 1986.

Lamott, Anne. *Bird by Bird: Some Instructions on Writing and Life.* New York: Anchor Books, 1994.

Levy, Mark. *Technicians of Ecstasy.* Connecticut: Bramble Books, 1993.

Maisel, Eric. *Affirmations for Artists.* New York: G. P. Putnam and Sons, 1996.

Ruddick, Sara, and Pamela Daniels. *Working It Out: 23 Women Writers, Artists, Scientists, and Scholars Talk About Their Lives and Work.* New York: Pantheon Books, 1977.

Framing and Shipping

Duren, Lista. *Frame It: A Complete Do-It-Yourself Guide to Picture Framing.* Boston: Houghton Mifflin Company, 1976.

Horne, Stephen. *Way to Go! Crating Artwork for Travel.* Hamilton, N.Y.: Gallery Association of New York State, 1985.

Grants and Residencies

Alliance of Artists' Communities. *Artists Communities: A Directory of Residencies in the United States Offering Time and Space for Creativity.* New York: Allworth Press, 1996.

Bowler, Gail Hellund. *Artists' and Writers' Colonies: Retreats, Residencies, and Respites for the Creative Mind.* Hillsboro, Ore.: Blue Heron Publishing, 1995.

Brunner, Helen M., Donald H. Russell, and Grant E. Samuelsen. *Money to Work II: Funding for Visual Artists.* Washington, D.C.: Art Resources International, 1992.

The Foundation Center. *Foundation Grants to In-*

dividuals. 10th ed. New York: The Foundation Center, 1997.

Gullong, Jane, and Noreen Tomassi, eds. *Money for International Exchange in the Arts.* New York: American Council for the Arts, 1992.

Lefferts, Robert. *Getting a Grant: How to Write Successful Grant Proposals.* Englewood Cliffs, N.J.: Prentice-Hall, 1978.

Oxenhorn, Douglas, ed. *Money for Visual Artists.* 2d ed. New York: American Council for the Arts, 1993.

Health Hazards

Michael McCann. *Health Hazards Manual for Artists.* New York: Lyons & Burford, 1994.

Rempel, Siegfried, and Wolfgang Rempel. *Health Hazards for Photographers.* New York: Lyons & Burford, 1992.

Shaw, Susan D., and Monona Rossol. *Overexposure, Health Hazards in Photography.* 2d ed. New York: Allworth Press, 1991.

Legal Issues

Conner, Floyd. *The Artist's Friendly Legal Guide.* Cincinnati: North Light Books, 1988.

Register of Copyrights. *Copyright Information Kit #115.* Washington D.C.: Library of Congress, 202-707-9100. Copyright information kit for visual artists; can be ordered by phone.

Crawford, Tad. *Legal Guide for the Visual Artist: The Professional's Handbook.* New York: Madison Square Press, 1986.

Hanson, Jo. *Artist's Taxes, The Hands-on Guide: An Alternative to Hobby Taxes.* San Francisco: Vortex Press, 1987.

Victoroff, Gregory. *The Visual Artist's Business and Legal Guide.* Englewood Cliffs, N.J.: Prentice-Hall, 1995.

Marketing and Publicity

Abbott, Susan, and Barbara Webb. *Fine Art Publicity.* Stamford, Conn.: The Art Business News Library, 1991.

Blakeslee, Carolyn, ed. *Getting Exposure: The Artist's Guide to Exhibiting the Work.* Upper

Fairmount, Maryland: Art Calendar Publishing, 1995.

Blakeslee, Carolyn, and Drew Steis, eds. *Making a Living as an Artist*. Upper Fairmount, Maryland: Art Calendar Publishing, 1993.

Caplin, Lee Evan, ed. *The Business of Art*. Englewood Cliffs, N.J.: Prentice-Hall, 1982.

Caputo, Kathryn. *How to Start Making Money with Your Crafts*. Cincinnati: Betterway Books, 1995.

Cox, Mary, ed. *Artist's & Graphic Designer's Market 1996*. Cincinnati: Writer's Digest Books, 1995.

DeVries, Henry, and Diane Gage. *Self-Marketing Secrets: Winning By Making Your Name Known*. San Diego: Pfeiffer & Company, 1991.

Fisher, Roger, and William Ury. *Getting to Yes: Negotiating Agreement Without Giving In*. New York: Penguin Books, 1991.

Hoover, Deborah A. *Supporting Yourself as an Artist: A Practical Guide*. New York: Oxford University Press, 1985.

Jackson, Zella. *The Art of Selling Art*. New York: The Consultant Press, 1988.

Klayman, Toby Judith, and Cobbett Steinberg. *The Artist's Survival Manual: A Complete Guide to Marketing Your Work*. Updated edition. New York: Charles Scribner's Sons, 1987.

Kostabi, Mark. *Conversations with Kostabi*. Rutland, Vermont: Charles E. Tuttle Co., Journey Editions, 1996.

Marx, Kathryn. *Photography for the Art Market*. New York: Amphoto, 1988.

Michels, Carroll. *How to Survive & Prosper As an Artist*. New York: Holt, Rinehart and Winston, 1983.

Nordling, Lee. *Your Career in the Comics*. Kansas City: Andrews and McMeel, 1995.

Ray, Michael, and Rochelle Myers. *Creativity in Business*. New York: Doubleday, 1986.

Reid, Sheila. *Art without Rejection*. Vence, France: Rush Editions, 1993.

Smith, Constance. *Art Marketing 101: A Handbook for the Fine Artist*. 2d ed. Penn Valley, Calif.: ArtNetwork, 1997.

The Crafts Center. *The Business of Crafts*. New York: Watson-Guptill Publications, 1996.

Vitali, Julius. *The Fine Artist's Guide to Marketing and Self-Promotion*. New York: Allworth Press, 1996.

Resources and Listings

Grant, Daniel. *The Artist's Resource Handbook*. Rev. ed. New York: Allworth Press, 1996.

Hiraki, Osam, and Maya Ishiwata, eds. *Japanese Photography Guide*. Tucson: Nazareli Press, 1996.

Howarth, Shirley Reiff. *Directory of Corporate Art Collections*. Largo, Fla.: International Art Alliance, 1984.

Jay, Bill, and Aimee Linhoff, eds. *USA Photography Guide*. Tucson: Nazareli Press, 1993.

Merz, Blanchard. *Art Year*. Torino, Italy: Hopefulmonster Editore, 1996.

Newbauer, Bernd, ed. *European Photography Guide*. Tucson: Nazareli Press, 1996.

Phillips, Renee. *New York Contemporary Art Galleries: The Complete Annual Guide*. 2d ed. New York: Manhattan Arts, 1997.

Rappaport, Susan S., and Victora Solan. *1996 Traveler's Guide to Art Museum Exhibitions*. New York: Harry N. Abrams, 1996.

Relyea, Lane. *Organizing Artists: A Document and Directory of the National Association of Artists' Organizations*. Washington, D.C.: National Association of Artists' Organizations, 1992.

Smith, Constance, ed. *ArtNetwork Yellow Pages*. Penn Valley, Calif.: ArtNetwork, 1995.

Writer's Digest Books. *Artist's & Graphic Designer's Market*. Cincinnati: F&W Publications 1997.

Slides

Titus, William. *Photographing Works of Art*. New York: Watson-Guptill Publications, 1981.

Studios

Kartes, Cheryl. *Creating Space: A Guide to Real Estate Development for Artists*. New York: American Council for the Arts, 1993.

Appendix II

Art Periodicals

Afterimage
31 Prince Street
Rochester, NY 14607
(716) 442-8676
Bimonthly magazine on photography, video, and film.

American Artist
1515 Broadway
New York, NY 10036
(212) 536-5165; fax (212) 536-5351
Subscriptions: One Color Court, Marion, OH 43305
Monthly focusing on the practicing artist; sales, galleries, grants; annual listing of art schools.

American Craft
American Craft Council
72 Spring Street
New York, NY 10012-4019
(212) 274-0630; fax (212) 274-0650

Aperture
20 East 23rd Steet
New York, NY 10010
Quarterly on photography.

ARIS Funding Reports: Creative Arts and Humanities Report
Academic Research Information System
2940 16th Street #314
San Francisco, CA 94103
(415) 558-8133
E-mail: arisnet@dnai.com
Web site: http://www.arisnet.com
Newsletter published eight times/year on current grants, fellowships, residencies, contests, and awards. Includes federal government and private sources.

Art and Australia
Fine Arts Press Pty., Ltd.
653 Pacific Highway, Suite 2
Killara 2071, Australia
Auction, artist and gallery coverage.

Art Calendar
P.O. Box 199
Upper Fairmount, MD 21867-0199
(410) 651-9150; (800) 597-5988; fax (410) 651-5313
Monthly listings of exhibition opportunities, competitions, grants. Published monthly except August.

Art in America
Brant Publications, Inc.
575 Broadway
New York, NY 10012
Subscriptions: P.O. Box 37003, Boone, IA 50037-0003; (800) 925-8059
General purpose monthly on U.S. scene; includes performing arts as well as visual arts.
Art in America, Annual Guide to Museums, Galleries and Artists
Published every August; remarkably accurate and informative.

Art International
Archive Press
77, Rue des Archives
Paris 75003, France
Beautiful magazine with short articles; for a general audience.

Art New England
Art New England Inc.
425 Washington Street
Brighton, MA 02135
(617) 782-4184
Bimonthly newspaper covering New England

and New York; guides to galleries and dealers, calendar of events, and reviews.

Art Now Gallery Guides
P.O. Box 5541
Clinton, NJ 08809
(908) 638-5255
U.S. regional plus international editions.

Art Papers
Atlanta Art Papers, Inc.
P.O. Box 77348
Atlanta, GA 30357
(404) 588-1837; fax (404) 588-1836
Theme-centered bimonthly on art world.

Art Year
Hopefulmonster Editore
Torino, Italy
Published twice yearly. Guide to exhibitions of art and architecture in museums throughout the world.

Artefactum
Amerikalei 125
B-2000 Antwerp, Belgium
Multilingual magazine on European scene; published five times/year.

Artforum
Department AF, P.O. Box 3000
Denville, NJ 07834-9828
(212) 475-4000
Visually exciting magazine (ten times yearly) on New York and international art scene; articles often theoretical, avant-garde; for serious contemporary artists, collectors, and curators.

Artist's Magazine
1507 Dana Avenue
Cincinnati, OH 45207
(513) 531-2222; (800) 283-0963; fax (513) 531-1843; (513) 531-2902

Subscriptions: P.O. Box 2120, Harlan, IA 51593
How-to magazine for working artists.

ArtNetwork (a publisher of marketing and career guides)
18757 Wildflower Drive
P.O. Box 1268
Penn Valley, CA 95946
(916) 470-0862; fax (916) 432-7633
Newsletters (*Artworld Hotline, Artsource Quarterly*), books (*ArtNetwork Yellow Pages, Art Marketing 101, Art Marketing Sourcebook for the Fine Artist*), and mailing lists (many categories).

ArtNews
ArtNews Associates
48 West 38th Street
New York, NY 1001
(212) 398-1690
Subscriptions: P.O. Box 2083, Knoxville, IA 50138-2083
Monthly, covering U.S. art scene.

Artweek
2149 Paragon Drive, Suite 100
San Jose, CA 95131-1312
(408) 441-7065; in CA (800) 733-2916
Monthly West Coast magazine.

Blindspot
c/o Lexington Photo Labs
49 West 23rd Street
New York, NY 10010
(212) 645-6155; fax (212) 691-5465
Semiannual photo magazine.

C Magazine
P.O. Box 5, Station B
Toronto, Ontario M5T 2T2, Canada
(416) 539-9495
Canadian art scene.

Camerawork
15 Natoma Street
San Francisco, CA 94105-3703
Published by Camerawork gallery.

Canadian Art
70 The Esplanade, 2nd Floor
Toronto, Ontario M5E 1R2, Canada
(416) 368-8854; fax (416) 368-6135
Subscriptions: 35 Riviera Drive #17, Markham,
    Ontario L34 8N4, Canada
Magazine on all types of Canadian visual art;
    "Focus" feature profiles a single artist with a
    large color print of work.

Drawing
The Drawing Society
15 Penn Plaza
Box 66
415 Seventh Avenue
New York, NY 10001
(212) 563-4822; fax (212) 563-4829
Articles and reviews focusing on drawing.

Fiberarts
50 College Street
Ashevile, NC 28801
(704) 253-0467; (704) 253-7952
Bimonthly covering textiles.

Flash Art International
Giancarlo Politi Editore
68 Via Carlo Farini
20159 Milan, Italy
Subscriptions: European Publications,
    799 Broadway, Rm. 237, New York, NY
    10003
Coverage of European and U.S. contemporary
    art.

Marg
Marg Publications
Army & Navy Building
148 Mahatma Gandhi Road

Bombay 400 023, India
Magazine on Indian art of all types.

Mediamatic
Stichting Mediamatic
Binnenkadijk 191, 1018ZE
Amsterdam, The Netherlands
Journal in Dutch and English on electronic
    media, especially video; technical articles; and
    reviews.

*New York Contemporary Art Galleries: The Com-
    plete Annual Guide*
Manhattan Arts International
200 East 72nd Street #26L
New York, NY 10021
(212) 472-1660

*Ocular: The Journal of Information & Opportunities
    for the Visual Art*
1539 Platte Street
Denver, CO 80202
Published quarterly.

Parkett
Parkett-Verlag AG
Quellenstrasse 27,
CH-8005
Zurich, Switzerland
Subscriptions: 14 West Tenth Street, New York,
    NY 10011
Beautiful bilingual quarterly focusing on one
    artist; articles and essays.

Photo Metro
17 Tehama Street
San Francisco, CA 94105
Ten times/year.

Photographers International
Bernhard DeBoer, Inc.
113 East Centre Street
Nutley, NJ 07110

Photography in New York International
64 West 89th Street
New York, NY 10024
(212) 787-0401; fax (212) 799-3054
Bimonthly.

PhotoTechnik International
Rupert-Mayer Strasse 45
D-81379 Munchen, Germany

Print
RC Publication
104 Fifth Avenue, 9th floor
New York, NY 10011
(212) 463-0600

Sculptors International Magazine & Sculpture
International Sculpture Center
1050 7th Street NW, Suite 250
Washington, DC 20036
Bimonthly magazines on American and international scene; information on commissions; published by the International Sculpture Center.

Southwest Art
CBH Publishing, Inc.
5444 Westheimer, Suite 1440
Houston, TX 77056
(713) 296-7900
Subscriptions: P.O. Box 1986, Marion, OH 43306

Nonspecialized magazine covering Southwest and California; interviews with artists.

Spot
Houston Center for Photography
1441 West Alabama
Houston, TX 77006
(713) 529-4755; fax (713) 529-9248
Twice yearly.

Studio
Givat Haviva
M.P. Menashe 37850, Israel
Monthly Hebrew language magazine covering Israel primarily, also U.S. and Europe; issues devoted to themes; some issues profile one prominent artist; articles and interviews.

Studio International
Medical Tribune Group
Tower House, 4th Floor
Southampton Street
LondonWC2E 7LS, England
Quarterly covering well-known contemporary international artists; essays and reviews.

StudioNOTES
Box 502
Benicia, CA 94510
(707) 746-55516
Northern California newsletter.

Appendix III

Organizations of Help to Artists

American Craft Association
21 South Eltings Corner Road
Highland, NY 12528
(914) 883-5218; fax (914) 883-6130
Artist membership group within American Craft

Council; health and property/casualty insurance; merchant credit card program; discounts on shipping and car rentals, long distance phone rates, magazine subscriptions; copublisher of *The Voice*, bimonthly newsletter; American Craft Information Center archive and database.

American Craft Council
72 Spring, Street
New York, NY 10012-4019
(212) 274-0630; fax (212) 274-0650
American Craft magazine; juried wholesale and
retail shows; slide registry; group rates on insurance; copublisher of *The Voice*, bimonthly
newsletter; discounts on subscriptions and
rentals and long distance phone rates; listing
in ACC database.

American Institute of Graphic Arts
164 Fifth Avenue
New York, NY 10010
(212) 807-1990; http://www.aiga.org
Promotes graphic design in books and other
media; 9,000 members nationally in 38 chapters; exhibitions, seminars, journals, publications; group rates on insurance.

American Society of Artists, Inc.
P.O. Box 1326
Palatine, IL 60078
(312) 751-2500; (847) 991-4748
National organization; quarterly newsletter, *Arti-
san;* art and craft shows; lecture, demo book-
ing service and publicity.

American Society of Media Photographers
(ASMP) National
14 Washington Road, Suite 502
Princeton Junction, NJ 08550
(609) 799-8300
(Call for local chapters)
Trade organization for print and electronic
photographers.

Americans for the Arts (formerly American
Council for the Arts)
1 East 53rd Street, 5th Floor
New York, NY 10022
(212) 223-2787; fax (212) 980-4857
and
927 15th Street NW
12th Floor
Washington, DC 20005

(202) 371-2830; fax (202) 371-0424
(800) 232-2789 hotline for information on
funding, insurance and books.

Art PAC
Bob Bedard
408 3rd Street SE
Washington, DC 20003
(202) 546-1804
Political action committee working for legislation benefitting individual artists.

Artist's Alliance of California
P.O. Box 2424
Nevada City, CA 95959
(916) 272-7357
Discounts on art materials; health insurance at
guaranteed rates; newsletter; discounted dental and legal and accounting services, museum memberships, computer equipment,
bookstore and travel services.

Artists in Print (AIP)
665 Third Street, Suite 530
San Francisco, CA 94107
(415) 243-8244; fax (415) 495-3155

Artists' Space/Committee for the Visual Arts, Inc.
38 Green Street, 3rd Floor
New York, NY 10013
(212) 226-3970; fax (212) 966-1939
Nonprofit gallery for emerging artists; slide registry being updated to photo CD.

Arts Midwest
528 Hennepin Avenue, Suite 310
Minneapolis, MN 55403
(612) 341-0755; fax (612) 341-0902

Association of Hispanic Arts, Inc.
173 East 116th Street, 2nd Floor
New York, NY 10029
(212) 860-5445
Latino arts-service organization serving primarily New York; information, technical help,
workshops, seminars, newsletter, grants to

New York arts organizations, publications including the *Directory of Hispanic Artists and Organizations.*

ATLATL
P.O. Box 34090
Phoenix, AZ 85067-4090
(602) 277-3711; fax (602) 277-3690
National Native American art service organization; artist registry, resource file; *Native Arts Update,* quarterly newsletter, technical assistance.

Boston Visual Artists Union, Inc. (BVAU)
P.O. Box 399
Newtonville, MA 02160
(617) 695-1266
Co-op gallery, slide registry, job bank file, and newsletter.

Chicago Artists' Coalition
11 East Hubbard Street 7th Floor
Chicago, IL 60611
(312) 670-2060
Artist-run service organization with newsletter.

Cityarts, Inc.
525 Broadway, Suite 700
New York, NY 10012
(212) 966-0377
Nonprofit public art organization specializing in murals.

College Art Association
275 Seventh Avenue, 5th Floor
New York, NY 10001
(212) 691-1051; fax (212) 627-2381
Publishes listings of college and museum art jobs; career placement service; annual conference for educators; group medical and life insurance; *Art Bulletin* and *Art Journal.*

Cultural Alliance of Greater Washington
1436 U Street NW, Suite 103
Washington, DC 20009-3997
(202) 638-2406

Job bank, health insurance; PR and accounting help; discount art and office supplies; monthly workshops.

Division of Civil Rights
National Endowment for the Arts
100 Pennsylvania Ave. NW, Room 812
Washington, DC 20506
(202) 682-5454
Directory of Minority Arts Organizations.

General Services Administration
Art in Architecture Program
18th & F Streets, NW
Washington, DC 20405
(202) 708-5082
Commission art for public buildings and slide registry.

Graphic Artists Guild
90 John Street, Room 403
New York, NY 10038
(212) 791-3400; fax (212) 791-0333;
http://www.gag.org
Published pricing guidelines for manual and digital art; lobbying for artists; group health insurance, discounts on car rentals, art supplies; dispute resolution.

International Sculpture Center
1050 17th Street NW, Suite 250
Washington, DC 20036
(202) 785-1144; fax (202) 785-0810
Sculpture magazine, member opportunities, discounts, conferences, lectures, art insurance, and upcoming World Wide Web slide registry.

National Artists Equity Association, Inc.
1725 K Street NW, Suite 1003
Washington, DC 20006
(202) 628-9633; or
3726 Albemarle Street NW
Washington, DC 20016
Branches across U.S.; newsletter, group insurance; business and legal help.

New York Artists' Equity Association
498 Broome Street
New York, NY 10013-2213
(212) 941-0130
Independent organization not connected with
National Artists' Equity; serves 3,000 artists
primarily New York, New Jersey, Conneticut;
exhibition space available for rent; tax and
legal information, slide file, quarterly publication, medical and dental plans, Welfare Fund
(interest-free loans to needy artists).

New York Foundation for the Arts
155 Avenue of the Americas, 14th floor
New York, NY 10013
(212) 366-6900; fax (212) 366-1778
Artists' Fellowships for New York state residents,
stipends; National Dance Residency Program;
financial services for artists and arts organizations; artist in residence awards; *FYI*, quarterly newsletter, ArtsWire, on-line art
information, Visual Artist Information
Hotline. Maintains list of New York area
arts organizations providing resources
for artists.

New York Graphic Society
P.O. Box 1469
Greenwich, CT 00836-1469

(203) 661-2400; (800) 677-6947;
fax (203) 661-2480

Packing and Crating Information Network
(PACIN, part of American Association of Museums)
Brent Powell, Chairman
c/o Nelson Atkins Museum of Art
4525 Oak Street
Kansas City, MO 64111
(816) 751-1294
Softpacking and other books on professional crating, shipping, risk assessment, insurance
available.

Printed Matter, Inc.
77 Wooster Street
New York, NY 10012
(212) 925-0325; fax (212) 925-0464
Bookstore and gallery for artists' books; mail
order catalogue; wholesale and retail.

Society of Illustrators
128 East 63rd Street
New York, NY 10021
(212) 838-2560
International organization of illustrators, photographers, art directors; gallery; annual best
illustration book.

Appendix IV

Grants and Residencies

Grantmaking Entities and Information

Artists Fellowship Inc.
c/o Salmagundi Club
47 Fifth Avenue
New York, NY 10003
(212) 255-7740
Grants during distress due to disability.

ARTS, Inc.
315 West 9th Street, Suite 201

Los Angeles, CA 90015
(213) 627-9276; fax (213) 627-9914
Reference library.

California Community Foundation
606 South Olive Street, Suite 2400
Los Angeles, CA 90014
(213) 383-2046; http://www.calfund.org
Artists in the greater LA area.

Blanche E. Colman Trust
c/o Boston Safe Deposit & Trust Co.

One Boston Place
Boston, MA 02108
(617) 722-6818
Artists from northeast recommended.

The Elizabeth Foundation for the Arts
P.O. Box 2670
New York, NY 10108
(212) 956-6633

Foundation Center
(800) 424-9836
(information on foundation funding, grants,
    and how to write proposals):
1001 Connecticut Avenue NW, Suite 938
    Washington, DC 20036
    (202) 331-1400
Kent H. Smith Library
    1422 Euclid, Suite 1356
    Cleveland, OH 44115
    (216) 861-1933
Suite 150, Grand Lobby, Hurt Building
    50 Hurt Plaza
    Atlanta, GA 30303
    (404) 880-0094
79 Fifth Avenue, 8th Floor
    New York, NY 10003
    (212) 620-4230
312 Sutter Street
    San Francisco, CA 94108
    (415) 397-0902

Foundation for Contemporary Performance
    Arts, Inc.
151 East 63rd Street
New York, NY 10021
(212) 308-6032
Grants by nomination only—foundation invites
    grants annually.

Adolph and Ester Gottlieb Foundation, Inc.
c/o Sandford Hirsch, Secretary-Treasurer
380 West Broadway
New York, NY 10012
(212) 226-0581
Painters, sculptors, printmakers with at least 20

years' experience; in mature phase of their art.
Emergency assistance for same with 10 years
of mature art.

Grantsmanship Center
1125 West 6th Steet, 5th Floor
Los Angeles, CA 90017
(213) 482-9860

John Simon Guggenheim Memorial Foundation
90 Park Ave, 33rd Floor
New York, NY 10016
(212) 687-4470

Jerome Foundation
West 1050 First National Bank Building
332 Minnesota Street
St. Paul, MN 55101-1312
(612) 224-9431
New York City and Twin Cities resident artists.

Kansas Cultural Trust
225 North Roosevelt
Wichita, KS 67208
(800) 666-9040
Current or former Kansas residents, or graduates
    of Kansas state university/colleges.

Kentucky Foundation for Women, Inc.
1215 Heyburn Building
332 West Broadway
Louisville, KY 40202
(502) 562-0045
Women artists living or working in Kentucky.

Emory and Ilona Ladanyi Foundation, Inc.
12 Ranch Place
Merrick, NY 11566
Grants to young American artists.

Materials for the Arts
New York City Department of Cultural Affairs
2 Columbus Circle
New York, NY 10019
(212) 841-4100; (212) 974-1150
Collects and distributes materials and equip-
    ment to art organizations.

MacDowell Colony
100 High Street
Peterborough, NH 03458
(603) 924-3886; fax (603) 924-9142
163 East 82nd Street
New York, NY 10028
(212) 535-9690; fax (212) 737-3803

Money for Women/Barbara Fund, Inc.
P.O. Box 40-1043
Brooklyn, NY 11240-1043
Project support for individual American or
    Canadian feminists in the arts.

National Sculpture Society, Inc.
1177 Avenue of the Americas, 15th Floor
New York, NY 10036
(212) 764-5645; fax (212) 764-5651

The Pollock-Krasner Foundation, Inc.
725 Park Avenue
New York, NY 10021
(212) 517-5400; fax (212) 288-2836
Grants to working painters, printmakers and
    sculptors.

Ludwig Vogelstein Foundation
P.O. Box 277
Hancock, ME 04640
Grants for specific projects.

The Wheeler Foundation, Inc.
126 West 11th St., Suite 24
New York, NY 10011
(212) 807-1915; fax (212) 929-7945
Fellowships and emergency grants to visual
    artists of color over 21 residing in New York
    City tri-state area.

Artists' Residencies
Edward Albee Foundation, Inc.
c/o William Flanagan Memorial Creative Persons
    Center
14 Harrison Street
New York, NY 10013

(212) 226-2020
One-month residencies for sculptors, visual
    artists, writers, and composers.

Alternative Worksite/Bemis Center for Contem-
    porary Arts
724 South 12th Street
Omaha, NE 68102
(402) 341-7130

American Academy in Rome
7 East 60th Street
New York, NY 10022-1001
(212) 751-7200

Arts International
Institute of International Education
809 United Nations Plaza
New York, NY 10017-3580
(212) 984-5370; fax (212) 984-5574

Bellagio Study Center
Rockefeller Foundation
420 Fifth Avenue
New York, NY 10018-2702
E-mail: bellagio@rockfound.org

The Djerassi Resident Artists Program
2325 Bear Gulch Rd.
Woodside, CA 94062-4405
(415) 747-1250
E-mail: drap@djerassi.com

Flintridge Foundation Visual Artists Award
1040 Lincoln Avenue, Suite 100
Pasadena, CA 91103
(626) 449-0839; fax (626) 585-0011
Primary residence must be in California, Ore-
    gon, or Washington for the last 3 years; mini-
    mum 20 years' work.

Northwood University Alden B. Dow Creativity
    Center
3225 Cook Road
Midland, MI 48640-2398
(517) 837-4478; fax (517) 837-4468

Partners of the Americas
1424 K Street NW, Suite 700
Washington, D.C. 20005
(202) 628-3300; fax (202) 628-3306
E-mail: info@partners.poa.com

The Helene Wurlitzer Foundation of New Mexico
P.O. Box 545
Taos, NM 87571
(505) 758-2413
Artists of all media; rent- and utilities-free housing in Taos.

Internet Resources

American Council for the Arts
Visual Artist Hotline
http://www.artsusa.org/hotline/vhlindex.htm
Information and services for artists, including funding, accounting and tax assistance, public art programs, studio space, residencies, health insurance, legal help.

Art DEADLINES List
http://www.xensei.com/adl/
List of international competitions, contests, call for entries/papers, grants, scholarships, fellowships, jobs, internships. Paid subscribers receive about 200 items each month; free list contains less. Mailing address: Resources, Box 381067, Cambridge, MA 02238.

Art in the Public Interest
http://www.artswire.org/highperf/APIhome.html
Nonprofit organization providing information about artists, organizations, projects, and ideas that bridge artistic and social concerns.

Art Walker Project
http://www.artwalker.com/
Showcase for realistic paintings and drawings of specific places in the United States organized as a map. Fun to explore.

ArtCity
http://www.artcity.com/
Delivers exhibitions from fine art galleries online. *Art and Auction* magazine articles. Gallery row. Art Exchange.

ArtJob
http://www./westaf.org/artjob/
Published by the Western States Arts Federation. A biweekly newsletter bringing up-to-date national and international listings of arts employment and related opportunities.

Artnet Magazine
http://www.artnet.com/home.html
Provocative, up-to-the-minute art world news and articles.

ArtsWire
http://www.artswire.org/
Supported by the New York Foundation for the Arts. Online network with professional level access to current art world news, latest listings of grants, exhibition opportunities, and jobs in the arts. There is a subscription fee.

AS220
http://users.ids.net/~as220/home.html
Uncensored and unjuried forum for the arts. Provides exhibition and performing space to all Rhode Island artists, exposing the world to the "AS220 aesthetic," to "amuse, confuse, and abuse our audience."

Center for Safety in the Arts
http://www.tmn.com/1/Artswire/csa
Provides information on hazards and precautions in the arts.

Cheap Joe's Art Stuff
http://www.artscape.com/cheapjoe/
Just about everything in watercolor, oil, acrylic, and pastel, at discounted prices.

Dick Blick Art Materials
http://www.dickblick.com/
Over 20,000 items in stock for artists and art educators.

Dia Center for the Arts
http://www.diacenter.org/
Multi-disciplinary contemporary arts organization based in New York City. The name Dia, taken from the Greek word meaning "through," was chosen to suggest its role as the conduit or means for realizing extraordinary projects.

The Foundation Center
http://fdncenter.org/
Free nonprofit information clearinghouse to foster public understanding of the foundation field by collecting, organizing, analyzing, and disseminating information related to foundations and corporate giving. Provides help for grant seekers/makers, researchers, policymakers, the media, and the general public. Locations in New York, Washington, D.C., Atlanta, Cleveland, and San Francisco with professional reference librarians.

Guerrilla Girls Homepage
http://www.voyagerco.com/gg/
Self-described "conscience of the art world," illuminating gender- and race-based discrepancies in the art world with poignancy and humor.

The Gunk Foundation
http://www1.mhv.net/~gunk/
Charitable operating foundation, concentrating on supporting two types of projects—public arts projects and scholarly/artistic publications (through publishing arm of the Foundation).

International Directory of Art Libraries
http://aaln.org/ifla-idal/
Provided as a means to access over 3,000 libraries and library departments with specialized holdings in art, architecture, and archaeology throughout the world.

Internet for the Fine Arts
http://www.fine-art.com/
Network of artists, galleries, museums, organizations, and resources for the fine arts.

Mailing Lists
http://custwww.xensei.com/adl/mlc/
Comprehensive specialized mailing lists. Categories include: Galleries, Museums, Organizations, Stores, Renters & Buyers, and Colleges. Order from: Resources, Box 381067 Harvard Sq. Stn., Cambridge, MA 02238. (617) 628-9749; fax (617) 926-9519 E-mail: adl@rtuh.com

New England Foundation for the Arts
http://www.nefa.org/
Provides support for artists in creation of artistic, professional, and community development; technology, cultural facilities, and international exchange.

The New York Foundation for the Arts
http://www.artswire.org/artswire/nyfa.html
Forum for artists and public to interactively experience and understand the arts. Provides grants and services to individual artists and their organizations in all artistic disciplines.

Oregon Arts Commission Announcements
http://www.das.state.or.us/oac/announce.htm
Comprehensive monthly listing by the Oregon Arts Commission of competitions, grants and residencies. 775 Summer St NE, Salem, OR 97310. (503) 986-0082.

Society for Photographic Education
http://www.arts.ucsb.edu/SPE/

Gives listings of job, grant, and exhibitions opportunities, and SPE activities.

WESTAF
htttp://www.westaf.org
Publisher of ArtJob and a source for additional information on career development resources for both individual artists and art organizations in a variety of art fields.

International Sites

Art of Russia
http://www.artofrussia.com/
Information on contemporary Russian artists.

Artnet Italia
http://www.thru.com/art/
Presents selected Italian artists and their works with the objective of creating a connection.

Art Planet
http://www.artplanet.com/
Free comprehensive on-line fine art directory for Artists, Auction Houses, Galleries, Libraries, Museums, Exhibitions, Publishers, and other Fine Art Services.

Artvision
http://www.artvision.tm.fr/
European marketplace for Fine Arts and Antiques. Provides complete services and information for upcoming auctions, prices public auctions with illustrated on-line catalogues.

CultureNet
http://www.ffa.ucalgary.ca/
A window on Canadian culture. It is a home, signpost, and jumping-off point for Canadian artists, networks, and cultural organizations.

State Arts Councils

Your state's art agency will be able to tell you, better than almost anyone, about regional, state, county, city, and town art organizations.

Alaska State Council on the Arts
411 W 4th Avenue, Suite 1E
Anchorage, AK 99501
(907) 269-6610; fax (907) 269-6601
Email: asca@alaska.net

American Samoa Council on Culture, Arts
   & Humanities
Office of the Governor
Box 1540
Pago Pago, AS 97699
(011-684) 633-4347; fax (011-684) 633-2059

Arizona Commission on the Arts
417 West Roosevelt

Phoenix, AZ 85003
(602) 255-5882 or -5884; fax (602) 256-0282

Arkansas State Council for the Arts
1500 Tower Building
323 Center Street
Little Rock, AR 72201
(501) 324-9766; fax (501) 324-9154
E-mail: info@dah.state.ar.us

California Arts Council
1300 I Street, Suite 930
Sacramento, CA 95814
(916) 322-6555; (916) 322-9556

Colorado Council on the Arts & Humanities
Grant-Humphreys Mansion
750 Pennsylvania Street
Denver, CO 80203-0399
(303) 894-2617; fax (303) 894-2615

Commonwealth of Pennsylvania Council on
the Arts
Room 216 Finance Building
Harrisburg, PA 17120
(717) 787-6883; fax (717) 783-2538

Delaware Division of the Arts
State Office Building 5th Floor
820 North French Street
Wilmington, DE 19801
(302) 577-8278; fax (302) 577-6561
E-mail: delarts@tmn.com

District of Columbia Commission on the Arts
& Humanities
4115 12th Street NW, Suite 804
Washington, DC 20004
(202) 724-5613; fax (202) 724-4135

Florida Arts Council
Division of Cultural Affairs
The Capitol
Tallahassee, FL 32399-0250
(904) 487-2980; fax (904) 922-5259

Georgia Council for the Arts
530 Means Street NW, Suite 115
Atlanta, GA 30318
(404) 651-7931; fax (404) 651-7922

Guam Council on the Arts & Humanities
Office of the Governor
Box 2950
Agana, GU 96910
(011-671) 477-9845 or 477-7413; fax (011-
671) 477-5651

Idaho Commission on the Arts
Box 83720
Boise, ID 83720-0008
(208) 334-2119; fax (208) 334-2488

Illinois Arts Council
State of Illinois Center
100 West Randolph Street, Suite 10-500

Chicago, IL 60601
(312) 814-6750; fax (312) 814-1471

Indiana Arts Commission
Indiana Government Center South
402 West Washington Street, Room W072
Indianapolis, IN 46204-2741
(317) 232-1268; fax (317) 232-5595

Institute of Puerto Rican Culture
Apartado Postal 4184
San Juan, PR 00902-4184
(809) 724-3210; fax (809) 722-2033

Iowa Arts Council
Capitol Complex
600 East Locust
Des Moines, IA 50319
(515) 281-4451; fax (515) 242-6498

Kansas Arts Commission
Jayhawk Towers
700 SW Jackson, Suite 1004
Topeka, KS 66603-3758
(913) 296-3335; fax (913) 296-4989

Kentucky Arts Council
31 Fountain Place
Frankfort, KY 40601-1942
(502) 564-3757; fax (502) 564-2839

Louisiana Department of Culture, Recreation
& Tourism
Division of the Arts
1051 North 3rd Street
Box 44247
Baton Rouge, LA 70804
(504) 342-8180; fax (504) 342-8173

Maine Arts Commission
55 Capitol Street
State House Station 25
Augusta, ME 04333
(207) 287-2724; fax (207) 287-2335

Maryland State Arts Council
601 North Howard Street
Baltimore, MD 21201
(410) 333-8232; fax (410) 333-1062

Massachusetts Cultural Council
120 Boylston Street, 2nd Floor
Boston, MA 02116
(617) 727-3668; fax (617) 727-0044

Michigan Council for Arts and Cultural Affairs
1200 Sixth Street
Executive Plaza
Detroit, MI 48226
(313) 256-1136; fax (313) 256-3781

Minnesota State Arts Board
400 Sibley Street
St. Paul, MN 55101
(612) 297-2603; (800) 8MN-ARTS (800-866-
   2787); fax (612) 297-4304

Mississippi Arts Commission
239 North Lamar Street, Suite 207
Jackson, MS 39201-1311
(601) 359-6030; fax (601) 359-6008

Missouri Alliance for Arts Education
The Joseph White Building
1750 South Brentwood Boulevard, Suite 501
Brentwood, MO 63144-1315
(314) 962-1880; fax (314) 962-2689

Montana Arts Council
316 North Park Avenue
Room 252
Helena, MT 59620-2201
(406) 444-6430

Nebraska Arts Council
3838 Davenport Street
Omaha, NE 68131-2329
(402) 595-2122; fax (402) 595-2334

Nevada State Council on the Arts
602 North Curry Street

Carson City, NV 89703
(702) 687-6680; fax (702) 687-6688

New Jersey State Council on the Arts
20 West State Street
Trenton, NJ 08625
(609) 292-6130; fax (609) 989-1440

New Mexico Arts Division
228 East Palace Avenue
Santa Fe, NM 87501
(505) 827-6490; fax (505) 827-6043

New York State Council on the Arts
915 Broadway
New York, NY 10010
(212) 387-7139; fax (212) 387-7164

North Carolina Arts Council
Department of Cultural Resources
109 East Jones Street
Raleigh, NC 27601-2807
(919) 733-7897; fax (919) 733-4834

North Dakota Council on the Arts
418 East Broadway, Suite 70
Bismarck, ND 58501
(701) 328-3954; fax (701) 328-3963

Ohio Arts Council
727 East Main Street
Columbus, OH 43205
(614) 466-2613; fax (614) 466-4494

Oregon Arts Commission
775 Summer Street NE
Salem, OR 97310
(503) 986-0088; fax (503) 986-0260
E-mail: oregon.artscomm@state.or.us

Rhode Island State Council on the Arts
95 Cedar Street, Suite 103
Providence, RI 02903-1034
(401) 277-3880, fax (401) 521-1351

South Carolina Arts Commission
1800 Gervais Street
Columbia, SC 29201-3585
(803) 734-8689; fax (803) 734-8526

South Dakota Arts Council
800 Governors Drive
Pierre, SD 57501-2294
(605) 773-3131; fax (605) 773-6962
E-mail: sdac@tmn.com

State Arts Council of Oklahoma
Jim Thorpe Building Room 640
2101 North Lincoln Boulevard
Oklahoma City, OK 73105
(405) 521-2931; fax (405) 521-6418

State Foundation on Culture & the Arts
44 Merchant Street
Honolulu, HI 96813
(808) 586-0300; fax (808) 586-0308

Tennessee Arts Commission
401 Charlotte Avenue
Nashville, TN 37243-0780
(615) 741-1701; fax (615) 741-8559

Texas Commission on the Arts
Box 13406
Austin, TX 78711-3406
(512) 463-5535; fax (512) 475-2699

Utah Arts Council
617 East South Temple Street
Salt Lake City, UT 84102
(801) 236-7555; fax (801) 236-7556
E-mail: dadamson@email.state.ut.us

Vermont Council on the Arts
136 State Street, Drawer 33
Montpelier, VT 05633-6001
(802) 828-3291; fax (802) 828-3363

Virgin Islands Council on the Arts
41-42 Norre Gade, Second Floor
St. Thomas, VI 00802
(809) 774-5984; fax (809) 774-6206

Virginia Commission for the Arts
Lewis House, 2nd Floor
223 Governor Street
Richmond, VA 23219-2010
(804) 225-3132; fax (804) 225-4327

Washington State Arts Commission
234 East 8th Avenue
Box 42675
Olympia, WA 98504-2675
(360) 753-3860

West Virginia Commission on the Arts
Arts & Humanities Section
1900 Kanawha Boulevard East
Charleston, WV 25305
(304) 558-0220; fax (304) 558-2779

Wisconsin Arts Board
101 East Wilson Street, 1st Floor
Madison, WI 53702
(608) 266-0190; fax (608) 267-0380

Wyoming Council on the Arts
2320 Capitol Avenue
Cheyenne, WY 82002
(307) 777-7742; fax (307) 777-5499

Appendix VII

Resources for Artists

Art Materials by Mail Order

Archivart
P.O. Box 428
Goodridge, NJ 07075

(800) 804-8428
Archival materials

Binders Discount Art Center
1938 Euclid Avenue

Cleveland, OH 44115
(800) 877-3242

Black Forest
730 Redding, Suite 754
Cincinnati, OH 45237
(616) 328-4478
Discounted oils and brushes

CKS
1115 North LaBrea Avenue
Inglewood, CA 90302
(888) 257-5463
Stretcher bars

Daniel Smith Artists' Materials
4150 First Avenue South
P.O. Box 84268
Seattle, WA 98124-5568
(800) 426-6740; fax (800) 238-406
General art supplies

Exposures
1 Memory Lane
P.O. Box 3615
Oshkosh, WI 54903-3615
(800) 222-4947
Frames and storage systems

Fine Arts Stretcher Bars
1746A Berkeley Street
Santa Monica, CA 90404
(310) 586-9222

FLAX
P.O. Box 7216
San Francisco, CA 94120
(800) 547-7778
General art supplies

Gibson Displays
122 White Dogwood Lane
Statesvillle, NC 28677
(704) 873-8121
Print bins

Light Impressions
P.O. Box 940
439 Monroe Avenue
Rochester, NY 14603-0940
(800) 828-6216; fax (800) 828-5539
Archival materials, portfolios, slide sheets

Metropolitan Picture Framing
6959 Washington Avenue South
Edina, MN 55439
(800) 626-3139; (612) 941-6649; fax (612)
    941-6733
E-mail: metroframe@aol.com

Sinopia: Pigments and Materials
229 Valencia Street
San Francisco, CA 94103
(415) 621-2898; fax (415) 621-2897
Online catalogue: http://www.sinopia.com
Supplies for making custom paints and brushes

Sisyphus Art Supply
(800) 872-2545
Stretcher bars

20th Century Plastics
P.O. Box 2376
Brea, CA 92822
(800) 767-0777
Slide sheets

Twin Brook Professional Stretchers
RR 1 Box 5444
Lincolnville, ME 04849
(800) 856-1567; fax (207) 763-4271

Utrecht Art Supply
Main Office, 33 35th Street
Brooklyn, NY 11232
(800) 223-9132; (718) 768-2525
(also in New York, Chicago, Philadelphia, Berke-
    ley, Washington D.C., Chicago, West L.A.,
    San Francisco, Detroit, and Boston)

Utility
P.O. Box 217

Gardiner, NY 12525
(914) 255-9290; fax (914) 255-9293
Canvas

Williamsburg Art Materials
RR 1, Box 465E
East Meredith, NY 13757
(800) 293-9399; (607) 278-6154;
fax (607) 278-6254
Handmade paints and pigments

Art Shippers

A-1 Babber Packing and Crating
8231 West 3rd Street
Los Angeles, CA 90048
(213) 651-3241

Alan Reynolds
(510) 452-1876; Pager (510) 310-3347

American Worldwide Freight Services
5677 West Century Boulevard, Suite 945
Los Angeles International Airport
Los Angeles, CA 90045
(310) 410-4012

ArtCrate
113 E. Union Street
Pasadena, CA 91103
(213) 681-2401

Art Handlers
1570 Pacheco Street #E14
Santa Fe, NM 87501
(505) 982-0228

Art Handlers AZ
3030 N. Civic Center 1-A
Scottsdale, AZ 85251
(602) 947-6050; fax (602) 947-1790
(800) 253-0158 (CA, NM, CO, TX)

Art Moves Incorporated
225 NW 26th Street
Miami, FL 33127
(305) 576-7576; fax (305) 576-9912

Art Source International
1237 Pearl Street
Boulder, CO 80302
(303) 444-4080

Artech Inc.
2609 First Avenue
Seattle, WA 98121
(206) 728-8822; fax (206) 728-1521

Artlines
P.O. Box 4825
West Hills, CA 91308
(818) 884-4886

Atelier 4
83 Pearl Street
Brooklyn, NY 11201
(800) 625-4278; fax (718) 852-5723

Atthowe Fine Arts Services
3924 Market Street
Oakland, CA 94608
(510) 654-6816; fax (510) 654-2632

Complete Art Services
1711 North Lakeside Drive
Lake Worth, FL 33460
(561) 624-4060

Contemporary Installations
449 North Oak Street
Inglewood, CA 90302
(310) 673-7200

Cookes Crating Inc.
3124 East 11th Street
Los Angeles, CA 90023
(213) 268-5101; fax (213) 262-2001

Crate 88
4091 Redwood Avenue
Los Angeles, CA 90066
(310) 821-8558; fax (310) 306-3572

Craters & Freighters
325 Corey Way, Unit 115
South San Francisco, CA 94080
(415) 583-8555; (800) 736-3335 ext. 300;
fax (415) 583-8572

Crozier Fine Arts
525 West 20th Street
New York, NY 10010
(800) 822-2787; (212) 741-2024;
fax (212) 243-5209

D.A.D. Trucking
76 Varick Street
New York, NY 10013
(212) 226-0054; (212) 226-0107;
fax (212) 226-1070

Elwell Trucking
1420 Carroll Avenue
San Francisco, CA 94124
(415) 822-5500

Enclosures
P.O. Box 77326
San Francisco, CA 94107
(415) 826-3640; fax (415) 826-4499

Eric Smith Art Services
63 Bluxome Street
San Francisco, CA 94107
(415) 357-1158

Fine Art Express Inc.
San Francisco: 1455 Custer Street, San Fran-
    cisco, CA 94124; (415) 648-4790
Boston: 251 Heath Street, Boston, MA 02130;
    (617) 566-1155
New York: 35-00 47th Avenue, Long Island
    City, NY 11101; (718) 361-7357
Houston: 465 West 38th Street, Houston, TX
    77018; (713) 691-5461
Fort Worth: 7440 Whitehall, Fort Worth, TX
    76118; (817) 589-0855

Fine Art Shipping
1714 Euclid Street
Santa Monica, CA 90404
(800) 421-7464; fax (310) 581-6838

Gardner & White
21-44 44th Road
Long Island City, NY 11101
(718) 729-8877

Grosso Art Packers
1400 York Avenue
New York, NY 10021
(212) 734-8879; fax (212) 288-9009

ICON Group Inc.
417 North Sangamon
Chicago, IL 60622
(312) 733-4266

International Cargo Systems Inc.
Fine Art Division
P.O. Box 457
East Boston, MA 02128
(617) 561-1171

Judson Art Warehouse
49-20 Fifth Street
Long Island City, NY 11101
(718) 937-5500

LA Packing & Crating
5722 West Jefferson Blvd.
Los Angeles, CA 90016
(213) 937-2669

Legacy
1045 N. 10th Street
San Jose, CA 95112
(800) 827-0990

Lawrence Fine Arts
1062 Revere Avenue
San Francisco, CA 94124
(415) 467-3628, fax (415) 467-2415

Morart (More Specialized Art Transportation)
222 Bargen Turnpike
Ridgefield, Park NJ 07660
(201) 641-2500; fax (201) 641-2580

Museum Services
2921 Como Avenue SE
Minneapolis, MN 55413
(612) 378-1189
Outdoor rigging, conservation, general fine arts

Parma Movers Inc.
P.O. Box 1986
Cleveland, OH 44106
(216) 791-4747

Racine Berkow Associates
375 West Broadway
New York, NY 10013
(212) 243-2269

Ship/Art International
P.O. Box 1176
South San Francisco, CA 94083
(415) 952-0100; fax (415) 952-8958
Express shuttles, SF-LA-NY, worldwide trans-
    portation, insurance

Simon's
2714 Bayview Drive
Alameda, CA 94501
(510) 865-8614

Transport Consultants International
37 Elm Street #8
Westfield, NJ 07090
(800) 752-7002; (908) 789-8923

Three Way International
1120 Carlstad Drive
Sunnyvale, CA 54089
(408) 734-2605

US Art Co.
199 Turnpike Street

Stoughton, MA 02072
(800) 872-7826

West Coast Keating
9034 Sunset Blvd. Suite 107
Los Angeles, CA 90069

Packaging and Crating Supplies

Airfloat Systems
P.O. Box 229
110 Elizabeth Street
Tupelo, MS 38802
(800) 445-2580
Polyurethane-lined corrugated cardboard

Chiswick Trading
33 Union Avenue
Sudbury, MA 01776
(800) 225-8708

Consolidated Plastics Co.
8181 Darrow Road
Twinsburg, OH 44087
(800) 362-1000

Curatorial Assistance
113 East Union Street
Pasadena, CA 91103
(213) 681-2401

Masterpak
50 W. 57th Street, 9th Floor
New York, NY 1019
(800) 922-5522; fax (718) 937-6413
Crating and packing kits and supplies

National Bag Co.
2233 Old Mill Road
Hudson, OH 44236
(800) 247-6000

Packing and Crating Information Network
    (PACIN)
Brent Powell, Chairman
c/o The Nelson Atkins Museum of Art

4525 Oak Street
Kansas City, MO 64111
(816)751-1294; fax (816) 561-7154

Uline Shipping Supply Specialists
P.O. Box 568
Lake Bluff, IL 60044
(800) 295-5510; (846) 295-5510

Slide Duplicates

Citizens Photo
P.O. Box 15068
Portland, OR 97215
(503) 232-8501
Good and inexpensive duplicates

Holland Photo
(800) 477-4024

K&L Custom Photographics
222 East 44th Street
New York, NY 10017
(212) 661-5600

Modernage
1150 6th Avenue, 2nd Floor
New York, NY 0036
(212) 997-1800

Replichrome
89 5th Avenue, Room 903
New York, NY 003
(212) 929-0409

Sunset Color Labs
P.O. Box 46145
Los Angeles, CA 90046

Appendix VIII

Legal Help

American Arbitration Association
140 West 51st Street, 9th Floor
New York, NY 10020
(212) 484-4000

California Lawyers for the Arts (formerly Bay
   Area Lawyers for the Arts)
Fort Mason Center
Building C, Room 255
San Francisco, CA 94123
(415) 775-7200

California Lawyers for the Arts
1641 18th Street
Santa Monica, CA 90404
(310) 395-8893

Colorado Lawyers for the Arts
200 Grant Street, Suite 303E
Denver, CO 80203
(303) 722-7994

Connecticut Volunteer Lawyers for the Arts/
Connecticut Commission on the Arts
227 Lawrence Street
Hartford, CT 06106
(203) 566-4770

Fund for the Arts
623 West Main Street, 2nd Floor
Louisville, KY 40202
(502) 582-0100

Georgia Volunteer Lawyers for the Arts
141 Pryor Street, Suite 2030
Atlanta, GA 30303
(404) 525-6046

Huntington Arts Council
213 Main Street
Huntington, NY 11743
(516) 271-8423

Lawyers for the Creative Arts
213 West Institute Place, Suite 411

Chicago, IL 60610
(312) 944-2787

Louisiana Volunteer Lawyers for the Arts
c/o Arts Council of New Orleans
821 Gravier Street, Suite 600
New Orleans, LA 70112
(504) 523-1465

North Carolina Volunteer Lawyers for the Arts/
City of Raleigh Arts Commission
P.O. Box 590
Raleigh, NC 27602
(919) 831-6234

Philadelphia Volunteer Lawyers for the Arts
251 South 18th Street
Philadelphia, PA 19103
(215) 545-3385

San Diego Volunteer Lawyers and Accountants
    for the Arts
c/o Offices of Peter Karlen
1205 Prospect Street, Suite 400
La Jolla, CA 92037
(619) 454-9696

St. Louis Volunteer Lawyers and Accountants for
    the Arts
3540 Washington, 2nd Floor
St. Louis, MO 63103
(314) 652-2410; fax (314) 652-0011

Texas Accountants and Lawyers for the Arts
2917 Swiss Avenue
Dallas, TX 75204
(800) 526-8252

Visual Artists and Galleries Association
521 Fifth Avenue, Suite 800
New York, NY 10017
(212) 808-0616

Volunteer Lawyers for the Arts
1 East 53rd Street, 6th Floor
New York, NY 10022
(212) 319-2787
Legal assistance for free or fee. Divisions all
    over U.S. Newsletters, books, seminars, and
    classes.

Volunteer Lawyers for the Arts, D.C.
918 16th Street NW, Suite 503
Washington, DC 20006
(202) 429-0229

Volunteer Lawyers for the Arts Program
Albany-Schenectady League of Arts, Inc.
19 Clinton Avenue
Albany, NY 12207
(518) 449-5380

Washington Area Lawyers for the Arts
733 15th Street NW Suite 700
Washington, DC 20005
(202) 393-2826; fax (202) 393-4444

CALIFORNIA LAWYERS FOR THE ARTS
ARTIST-GALLERY AGREEMENT

This Agreement is made the _____ day of _____, _____ [year] by and between:

NAME: _____ ("Artist")

ADDRESS: _____

PHONE: _____

and

NAME: _____ ("Gallery")

ADDRESS: _____

PHONE: _____

Specify legal organization of gallery (e.g., corporation).

which is organized as a _____

The parties agree as follows:

Specify exclusive or non-exclusive agency and geographical area (e.g., San Francisco).

1. AGENCY. Artist appoints Gallery as his/her (exclusive/non-exclusive) agent for the purpose of exhibition and sale of the consigned works of art in the following geographical areas:

_____

2. CONSIGNMENT. Artist shall consign to Gallery and Gallery shall accept consignment of the following works of art during the term of this Agreement:

Include one of the following applicable statements, specifying particular media when appropriate.

- __ All new works created by Artist [in the following media: _____
_____]

- __ All works which Gallery shall select. Gallery shall have the first choice of all new works created by Artist [in the following media: _____
_____]

- __ Not less than _____ new works per year [in the following media: _____
_____]

- __ All new works created by Artist excluding works reserved by Artist for studio sales and commission sales made directly by Artist.

- __ The works described in the Consignment Sheet (Schedule A of this Agreement) and such additional works as shall be mutually agreed and described in a similar Consignment Sheet.

Artist shall not exhibit or sell any consigned work independently from Gallery without the prior written approval of Gallery. Artist shall be free to exhibit and sell any work not consigned to Gallery under this Agreement.

Specify Artist or Gallery.

3. DELIVERY. _____ shall be responsible for delivery of the consigned works to Gallery. All costs of delivery (including transportation and insurance) shall be paid as follows:

(a) _____% by Artist;   (b) _____% by Gallery.

4. TITLE & RECEIPT. Artist warrants that he/she created and possesses unencumbered title to all works of art consigned to Gallery under this Agreement. Title to the consigned work shall remain in Artist until he/she is paid in full. Gallery acknowledges receipt of the works described in the Consignment Sheet (Schedule A of this Agreement) and shall give Artist a similar Consignment Sheet to acknowledge receipt of all additional works consigned to Gallery under this Agreement.

Specify promotional efforts (e.g., exhibitions, openings).

5. PROMOTION. Gallery shall make reasonable and good faith efforts to promote Artist and to sell the consigned works as follows: _____
_____.

Specify discount percentage (if any).

6. SALES PRICE. Gallery shall sell the consigned works at the retail price mutually agreed upon by both parties and specified in writing in the attached Consignment Sheet. Gallery shall have discretion to vary the agreed retail price by _____% in the case of discount sales only.

Specify each art medium separately.

7. SALES COMMISSION. Gallery shall receive the following sales commission:
(a) _____% of the agreed retail price for selling works in the following medium: _____.
(b) _____% of the agreed retail price for selling works in the following medium: _____.
(c) _____% of the amount paid for studio sales or commission sales made directly by Artist.

Optional.

The remainder of the retail price shall be paid to Artist. In the case of discount sales, the amount of the discount shall be deducted from the Gallery's sales commission.

8. PAYMENT.
(a) On outright sales, Gallery shall pay Artist's share within thirty (30) days after the date of sale.
(b) On deferred payment sales, Gallery shall pay Artist's share within thirty (30) days after the transfer of possession of artwork or reciept of sales proceeds, whichever comes first.
(c) Installment sales must be approved in advance by the aritist and may not extend for a period of longer than six (6) months unless otherwise approved by the artist. On installment sales, Gallery shall first apply all proceeds from sale of the work to pay Artist's share. Payment shall be made within thirty (30) days after Gallery's receipt of each installment.

As provided by law, California Civil Code Section 1738.6 (d), Gallery shall hold the proceeds from the sale of consigned works in trust for the benefit of Artist. Gallery agrees to guarantee the credit of its customers, and to bear all losses due to the failure of the customer's credit.

9. APPROVAL SALES. Gallery shall not permit any consigned work to remain in the possession of a customer for the purpose of sale on approval for a period exceeding fourteen (14) days.

10. RENTALS. Gallery may not rent any consigned work without the prior written consent of Artist. The rental period may not exceed _____ weeks, unless a longer period is approved by Artist. Gallery shall receive _____% of the rental fees, and the remainder shall be paid to Artist within thirty (30) days after Gallery's receipt of each rental fee.

11. EXHIBITIONS. Gallery shall arrange, install, and publicize at least _____ [number] solo exhibitions of Artist's work on the main premises of Gallery of not less than _____ weeks duration each and within the initial term of this agreement. Gallery shall make reasonable efforts to arrange other solo and group exhibitions thereafter. Artist's work may not be included in any group exhibition without his/her prior written approval. Gallery shall be responsible for costs of exhibitions and other promotional efforts, including:

_____

_____

_____

_____

Consider costs of preparation, promotions, reception, framing, installation hardware, etc., when assigning responsibility for costs.

12. LOSS OR DAMAGE. As provided by law, California Civil Code Section 1738.6(c), Gallery shall be responsible for loss of or damage to the consigned work from the date of delivery to Gallery until the date of delivery to the purchaser or repossession by Artist. Gallery shall insure the consigned works for the benefit of Artist for _____% of the agreed retail price. In the event of damage to artwork, no restoration efforts shall be undertaken without the express advance consent of Artist, who shall have have first right to perform restoration.

13. STATEMENTS OF ACCOUNT. Gallery shall give Artist a Statement of Account (Schedule B of this Agreement) within fifteen (15) days after the end of each quarter of the calendar year, beginning with _____ [month] _____[year]. The Statement of Account shall include the following information:
(a) the work(s) sold or rented;
(b) the date, price, and terms of sale or rental;
(c) the commission due to Gallery;
(d) the name and address of each purchaser or renter;
(e) the amount due to Artist;
(f) the location of all unsold works (if not on Gallery's premises).

Gallery warrants that the Statement of Account shall be accurate and complete in all respects. With reasonable notice given Artist and Gallery (or their authorized representatives) shall have the mutual right to inspect the financial records of the other party pertaining to any transaction involving Artist's work.

14. CONTRACT FOR SALE. Gallery shall use Artist's own contract for sale in any sale of the consigned works.

15. COPYRIGHT. Artist reserves the common-law copyright to all works consigned to Gallery, including all reproduction rights and the right to claim statutory copyright. No work may be reproduced by Gallery without the prior written approval of Artist. All approved reproductions in catalogues, brochures, advertisements, and other promotional literature shall carry the following notice: © _____[year of publication] by _____ [name of Artist].

16. SECURITY. As provided by law, California Civil Code Section 1738.6(b), the consigned works shall be held in trust for the benefit of Artist, and shall not be subject to claim by a creditor of Gallery. In the event of any default by Gallery, Artist shall have all the rights of a secured party under the Uniform Commercial Code.

17. TERM OF AGREEMENT. This Agreement shall commence upon the date of signing and shall continue in effect until the _____ day of _____, _____. Thereafter, either party may terminate the Agreement by giving thirty (30) days prior written notice, except that the Agreement may not be terminated for ninety (90) days following a solo exhibition of Artist's work in Gallery. Artist has the right to terminate this agreement in the event of a Gallery close, move or bankruptcy.

Specify Artist or Gallery.

18. RETURN OF WORKS. _____ shall be responsible for return of all works not sold upon termination of the Agreement. All costs of return (including transportation and insurance) shall be paid as follows:
(a) _____% by Artist;   (b) _____% by Gallery.

If Artist fails to accept return of the works within ____ days after written request by Gallery, Artist shall pay reasonable storage costs.

19. NON-ASSIGNABILITY. The Agreement may not be assigned by Gallery to another person or gallery without the prior written approval of Artist. Gallery shall notify Artist in advance of any change in personnel in charge of Gallery or of any change in ownership of Gallery.

20. ARBITRATION. All disputes arising out of this Agreement shall be submitted to final and binding arbitration unless the parties otherwise agree to mediation of said dispute. The arbitrator or mediator shall be selected in accordance with the rules of Arts Arbitration and Mediation Services, a

program of California Lawyers for the Arts. If such service is not available, the dispute shall be submitted to arbitration in accordance with the laws of California. The arbitrator's award shall be final, and judgment may be entered upon it in any court having jurisdiction thereof. The prevailing party in the arbitration under this agreement shall be entitled to reasonable attorney's fees and costs incurred in the course of said arbitration.

21. ENTIRE AGREEMENT. This Agreement represents the entire agreement between Artist and Gallery and supersedes all prior negotiations, representations, and agreements, whether oral or written. This Agreement may only be amended by written instrument signed by both parties.

22. GOVERNING LAW. This Agreement shall be governed by the laws of the State of California.

IN WITNESS WHEREOF the parties hereto have executed this Agreement on the day and year first written above.

_____	_____
Artist	For Gallery

CONSIGNMENT SHEET (SCHEDULE A)

Received From: _____ Date: _____

The following works of art:

TITLE: MEDIUM: SIZE: RETAIL PRICE: RENTAL PRICE:

1. _____
2. _____
3. _____
4. _____
5. _____
6. _____
7. _____
8. _____
9. _____
10. _____

SIGNED BY:

_____   _____

  Artist   For Gallery

STATEMENT OF ACCOUNT (SCHEDULE B)

Artist: _____ Date: _____

Address: _____ Quarter: _____

TITLE: RETAIL PRICE: SALES COMMISSION: DUE TO ARTIST:

1. _____
2. _____
3. _____
4. _____
5. _____
6. _____
7. _____
8. _____
9. _____
10. _____

NET AMOUNT DUE TO ARTIST: $_____

_____

  For Gallery

Index

"Rediscovering Your Accomplishments" exercise, 30, 31
Rejections
  collecting, 81
  minimizing sting of, 80–81
  types of, 81–83
Resale royalty rights, 97
Residencies, 158, 170, 180–81
Reviews, 43
Richardson, Yancey, 104
Rights
  of Attribution, 92
  copyright, 79–80, 94–96
  exclusive, 14, 89
  of Integrity, 92, 93
  moral, 92–93, 97
  resale royalty, 97
  worldwide, 14, 89

• S
Shipping, 86–87, 117–20, 170, 188–91
Slides. See also Artist's packet
  book on, 172
  compiling sheet of, 43
  continual resending of, 81, 155–56
  duplicate, 52–53
  enclosing SASE for return of, 42
  essential characteristics of, 44–45
  hiring a professional photographer, 45–46
  importance of quality of, 44
  labeling, 53
  sending to consultants, 15
  sending to galleries, 24–25, 155–56
  shooting your own, 46–52
  slides out list, 104–6
  viewed by jurors, 66–67
Software, 103–4, 121
State arts councils, 183–86

Stationery, 42
Studios
  book on, 172
  getting, 164
  setting goals for time in, 61–62
Subway art, 20–21
Supplies, mail-order, 186–88
Support group, forming a, 161–63

• T
Talent, xiv–xv
Taxes, 121–22, 170–71
Taxicab gallery, 20
Taylor, Tim, 56
Technical skills, improving, xvii

• U
University galleries, 12
UPS, 119–20
USA Photography Guide, 77

• V •
VARA (Visual Artists Rights Act), 92–93, 97
Visual diary, xvii
Volunteer work, 156–57

• W
Washington, D.C., status of, 78
Way to Go, 118
Web sites. See Internet
White, Alexis, 38, 41
Work habits
  developing regular, 163–64
  importance of, xiv, xv
Worldwide rights, 14, 89

• Y
Yamrus, Frank, 155